Going Green

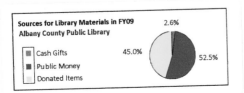

GOING GREEN

True Tales from Gleaners, Scavengers,
and Dumpster Divers

Edited by Laura Pritchett

UNIVERSITY OF OKLAHOMA PRESS : NORMAN

A portion of the proceeds from this book will be donated to the Rocky Mountain Land Library.

All photographs are by Andrew Gulliford unless otherwise indicated.

Library of Congress Cataloging-in-Publication Data

Going Green : true tales from gleaners, scavengers, and Dumpster divers / edited by Laura Pritchett.
   p.   cm.
  ISBN 978-0-8061-4013-1 (pbk. : alk. paper)
  1. Ragpickers—United States. 2. Salvage (Waste, etc.)—United States.
  3. Recycling (Waste, etc.)—United States.
  I. Pritchett, Laura, 1971–
  HD9975.U6G65 2009
  363.72'82—dc22

2008043176

The paper in this book meets the guidelines for permanence and durability of the committee on Production Guidelines for Book Longevity of the Council on Library Resources, Inc. ∞

This book is printed on FSC-certified Recycled Natural paper stock, which contains 30 percent post-consumer waste. The cover is printed on FSC-certified Kallima paper stock, which contains 10 percent post-consumer waste. Both text and cover were printed by FSC-certified printers.

1 2 3 4 5 6 7 8 9 10

Contents

Part 3. Teach Me: Gleaning for and from People

Preface

In one of my earliest memories, I am Dumpster diving. I am about five, standing on paper bags in a full Dumpster, and handing a silver necklace and a blender to my kid brothers, who are standing next to a little red wagon on the pavement below. We intend to use this wagon to haul our treasures home, and my heart is exploding with what I'll later learn is called "pride" as I look down at the blender and necklace that have just been tucked in among the other finds of the day. Some older brother or another (I can't remember which—they were all divers) is next to me in the Dumpster, showing us the ropes at this married-student-housing complex at the nearby university: watch out for glass, stay away from diapers, duck if a car drives by, smile cute if the cops come.

A few years later, when I was eight, my family moved to a ranch, and I was no longer near Dumpsters or the wonders they contained. But soon my kid brothers and I were sneaking into old abandoned houses to retrieve copper wiring, which we took to the "metal yard." Other times, we walked to the fairgrounds to collect beer and pop cans, which we'd smash, bag, and haul to the recycling center. My older brothers, who could drive, gave us their booty from diving—leather scraps, reams of paper, yards of nylon, bungee cords. We all loved finding things—arrowheads and blue bottles on the family ranch, cool rocks, clothes abandoned alongside the river. Always, we were seeking some sort of treasure.

I grew up in a household that encouraged this sort of behavior, and by that I mean not only retrieving good and valuable stuff but also living outside of the box. My mother, especially, fostered an independence and a mild scorn for authority (at least the authority of the human sort). We nine kids were not to care about fashion or that our clothes were secondhand; we were not to care what people thought when we climbed out of a Dumpster; we were not to live by rules that made no sense. For this, I am eternally grateful.

But soon my kid brothers and I were sneaking into old abandoned houses.

Somehow, though, I grew away from finding and salvaging things, and it wasn't until I was in my thirties that I found myself gleaning again on a fairly regular basis. My new friend, Tim, a Dumpster diver and geologist, rekindled my passion for finding stuff. If we weren't scratching around for clamshell fossils in the foothills of Colorado, we were looking for copper and redwood planks and sleeping bags from a Dumpster. And so it came to be, a year or so ago, while diving with Tim and my own five-year-old, that I first thought about the word "gleaning." I had some vague notion of people walking through a field after a harvest and women in big billowy dresses gathering up leftover crops. And I had an idea that it could mean more than that, too. But I had to look the word up to even find out what it meant exactly—which is, basically, reusing a resource after the "regulars" have used it.

After that, the word "gleaning" took on a whole new meaning. I started seeing it in action, as a verb, everywhere—in my kids' art projects, in their schools' classrooms, in my friends' homes, on my friends' dinner plates, in our conversations over dinner, and in the ways we learn from one another. I also started widening my own acceptance of gleaning—for example, I ate my first food from a Dumpster (pasta, cake mixes, chocolate), at first with some reluctance, then with gusto. I was already a fan of Goodwill, but after Dumpster diving, I declared Goodwill too expensive—the Dumpster stuff was free, after all. My two kids then became my regular compatriots, and with that there came kid questions: why do people throw this stuff away? If there are hungry people in the world, how come there's food in this Dumpster? Their simple questions, and the more complex answers they required, got me thinking. The more we gleaned, or talked about gleaning, the more I became interested in the ways our culture does—or does not—reuse its resources.

Gleaning, especially for food, is a revered occupation in some parts of the world. It is an inherently good thing to not let things go to waste. Not so in America. In my home state of Colorado, two fellows recently got jail time for getting produce out of a Dumpster in Steamboat Springs. It's illegal to glean from farmers' fields; We the People would rather, it seems, let that food rot than let individuals collect it. And while we lose tons of food in fields, we lose another enormous share at the counter—according to the USDA, about 96 billion pounds of edible food are lost each year by retailers and consumers, meaning that half the food produced in this country never gets eaten. This while people starve.

We are a country that prefers new to used, and we are a people who assume one would only reuse if one absolutely *needs* to. It is no surprise, then, that gleaning is associated with poverty. When I started researching this topic in earnest, I had to laugh at where "gleaning" is listed in the library catalogue—right alongside "homelessness," "social marginality," and "border areas." When my son told a student on the school bus that he sometimes Dumpster dived, the kid (unsurprisingly) teased him for being from a white-trash family.

"Are we white trash?" my son asked, in tears, as he tumbled off the bus and into my arms. *I don't know*, I thought, *maybe. It depends on how you define it.* And also, of course, I thought, *Does it matter?* We're firmly middle-class, and my husband and I are two PhDs with white-collar careers (though I am a writer, which makes me immediately suspect). So our diving is not out of necessity (thankfully); it's a deliberate choice—and I am aware that makes me privileged and a bit odd at the same time. I don't *have* to clothe myself and my kids with clothes from a Dumpster, or stock our house with toys, tools, and things from a Dumpster, but that's what I choose to do. I don't have to take my two kids Dumpster diving, but they like to go, and so do I.

I hugged my son there at the bus stop and mumbled a long trying-for-right parentish thing, something along the lines of "I don't know, but it doesn't matter, try not to listen to that kid, because I love us the way we are, and I hope you do too. It's so dang hard not to care about the way people judge us, but in fact, try not to care, and if we're happy, and we're doing good things, then that's all that really matters . . ."

A half an hour later, while eating his after-school snack, he asked when we could go diving. I laughed, and we went. We have a favorite route, my kids and I, alongside the backs of certain stores, into a neighborhood of fancy condos, then back to that same university housing I visited when I was five. As we drove and dived, I thought about the sad but true fact about how our family's status keeps us out of all sorts of trouble. The fact that we look the way we do—we are not homeless or a minority—keeps us safe. You can bet I get less hassle from the cops or store owners because I look like a white middle-class American in a Dumpster. Being a woman helps too. Having kids around is a plus. And psychologically, we are blessed too—we are able to have fun while gleaning, because we are not hell-bent on survival. I could feel guilty about that, I suppose, but I am who I am, and so instead I am grateful. All of which is only to say that gleaning—in many of its forms—is obviously tied to economics, social status, culture, and interesting concepts we have about what is okay for whom and why.

I wish this wasn't so. I wish things were different.

As soon as I thought those two lines—that very second—I knew I'd be putting together a book. Because, as a writer, desire fuels passion, and passion thumps away in my heart until I've turned it into words. So on the way home that afternoon, my car piled with found items (a yoga mat, a brand-new office chair slashed by the office supply store, a hundred envelopes, clothes, toys, and a copy of a Jane Austen book), I decided to do just that. I decided to ask others about their reasons, methods, and attitudes about gleaning. I wanted to see how their gleaning tied into bigger pictures of consumption, land use, healthy oceans, skies, and water. I wanted to see how gleaning was (or could be) pulled into the norm, the ways it can exist on the periphery, and the ways that we can all think about reusing resources every day. What I wanted, I think, was for there to come a day when my kid could say he Dumpster dives, and some other kid, from whatever social strata or ethnic group, could say, "Cool! Can I come along?"

This book contains some amazing essays that discuss not just the many ways people glean but the larger, more complex issues that occur alongside. Gleaning junk from a beach leads to a discussion of the enormous amount of plastic waste in our oceans. Picking up a pair of pants from a gutter leads to a discussion of this country's cotton industry. Finding a dead animal from the side of the road to eat leads to, well, raised eyebrows and a chuckle of admiration. Here are essays that not only explore reusing but explore our culture at large. How we use water, trash service, popsicle sticks. How and why people start Re/Stores for Habitat for Humanity or choose to save a dying woman's paintings. Some of the authors herein glean for survival. Others do it because they want to. Some are forced into it; others learn to love it. Some essays are pure delight, others will break your heart, and others will make you wonder if it's possible for you to change. All of them are concerned about what reusing (or not) says about our culture and our priorities.

This book is divided into three sections. The first is about gleaning items—food, turf grass, clothes, junk on a beach. In funny and moving and evocative ways, these authors show us how to see the world as a gleaning opportunity. The second section is about gleaning for or from our homes—whether it's dishwater or old wood or an old house itself, we find that our homes say a lot about who we are. Finally, the last section is about gleaning from other people—information, understanding, compassion—and perhaps most importantly, about finding the serious and intense ways in which we connect. There is plenty of overlap, of course; the interconnectedness of everything never ceases to amaze. This organization is not meant to separate but to allow for a conversation of sorts, where one piece flows into, and informs, another.

I hope you enjoy this book as much as I do. It's funny and light, serious and thoughtful, wise and humble. It's dedicated to all of you out there who glean, who believe in gleaning, and who hope for a world in which things find many, many uses.

I offer my most heartfelt thanks to the contributors for sharing their words, their varied ways of gleaning, and their hopes. I would also like to thank my husband, James, and my children, Jake and Eliana, for being good sports and generous souls. Thank you to my parents and siblings, and thanks to Tim Vaughan, Matthew Bokovoy, Jeff Lee, John Calderazzo, and Andrew Gulliford. Thanks also to every person out there who has found an item, considered it, and put it to a new use.

Laura Pritchett

PART ONE

Good Circulation

Gleaning Food and Things

Gleaning with Mac

LINDA M. HASSELSTROM

Raised on a South Dakota ranch, Linda M. Hasselstrom adjusted
her gleaning habits to fit the city when she moved to Cheyenne,
Wyoming. Her first Westie chased coyotes, but her current companion pursues squirrels and cats. Similarly, Linda's viewpoints
have diversified in fifteen years of city life. Linda has recently
returned to her South Dakota ranch, which is the site of the Great
Plains Native Plant Society's botanic garden and Windbreak House
writing retreat. Her many books of nonfiction include *Between
Grass and Sky*, and her most recent poetry collection is *Bitter
Creek Junction*.

I spotted the tall glass showcase in the alley a block from home
during my noon dog walk, hustled home for the car, and brought
home my fragile find in the passenger seat. The case was lovely, four
glass panels fitted into slender, polished oak struts, but neither my
partner, Jerry, nor I could think of a use for it.

Then, for his birthday, Jerry's sister gave him one of the oxygen
bottles she used while climbing Mount Everest. We draped the

battered orange canister with Tibetan prayer flags and propped it up in the trophy case as a symbol of her achievement. When guests look at the presentation, I usually manage to mention where I found the case.

The dog I walk down the alley with is recycled too.

Mac is a West Highland White Terrier (or Westie) who may have been five years old when he was put outside to "live free." His hair was so matted it couldn't be combed, so we had to shave him, and we found burrs buried in infected wounds in his flesh.

Walking Mac is my excuse, but what I've really been doing is gleaning the alleys around my city home for fifteen years. My neighbors would be shocked at how much I know about their lives from what they discard, and how many of their castoffs are now in my home.

Sure, I've saved money and our common resources by keeping useful objects out of the landfill. But the best part of alley gleaning is also the hardest to explain. I'm not just there to collect usable objects. I'm there to learn. When I started walking the alleys, I had two Westies. Watching them discover nuances of meaning I cannot share has improved my life every single day. No matter what disaster had befallen me, I laughed when their pink ears stood up and they bounced like merry-go-round horses to greet their canine neighbors. Delicately, they'd apply their noses to the fence slats or the holes in chain link or that tall bush. For them, each day was filled with possibility, with confidence that something wonderful would surely happen.

Counseled by the dogs, I've watched squirrels tinker with bird feeders, inspected alcoves where teenagers hide to smoke cigarettes, and heard the first blue jay of spring shatter the morning. While the dogs inhaled, collecting information for sheer delight, with no consideration for how they might use it, I also breathed deeply, pondering the essay or poems I'd worked on that morning, often finding an insight that might have eluded me if I hadn't taken time for the walk.

No matter what disaster had befallen me, I laughed when their pink ears stood up and they bounced like merry-go-round horses to greet their canine neighbors.

On the ranch where I grew up, I learned responsibility for every aspect of my life, from the garbage I created to the garden we tended, from cooking to cleaning out the septic tank. No one hauled our trash out of sight and mind; we buried it in our own pastures, so even as a child I was taught that avoiding waste was worth considerable effort. Living in the city, I follow old habits: compost, recycle, mulch, boil food scraps into dog food or soup stock.

So when I first walked in the alleys, I was horrified at what people threw away. The first thing I dragged home might have been the wicker chair with the wide, curved top. In such chairs, romantic novelists are photographed preening coyly in flouncy dresses, hair artfully arranged. I put the chair under the apple tree, arranged myself, and summoned Jerry with the camera, but I looked like a sunburned rancher who'd wandered into someone else's photo album.

What did we find next? The maple flooring? Maybe the plastic yard chairs, or the five mismatched but comfortable chairs that surround the secondhand dining room table. I've collected hundreds of flowerpots, some of them containing plants that still thrive in the porch, yard, and house, on plant stands, tables, and stools from the alley. I have found shovels, rakes, tomato cages and walls of water to protect them from frost, watering cans, rolls of fence wire, cake pans, dozens of canisters with tight-fitting lids, and rugs I use for mulch around trees and tomato plants. Occasionally, I've been incautious—an exotic plant I found discarded at the botanic garden was infested with critters, but soap and water spray killed them.

Though my partner and I brought to our relationship full sets of cooking utensils, there's no such thing as too much cast iron, so I reseasoned two rusty frying pans and added them to our camping supplies. The thrift store welcomed the children's playthings and clothing, and the dog toys I collected are still in the yard. The pictures I found weren't to my taste, but I use the foam board and frames. The inch-high silver caribou is on a shelf, and I added the windmill pin to my western hat, interpreting it as a symbolic message of hope to a displaced rancher and writer.

Though we haven't found a use for the piano innards, we're fascinated by the intricate mechanism of the soundboard, the shape of the muffler felt on the slender hammers, and the way the damper lifts from each wire string so it can sing. The simple black and white keyboard hides the maze that produces the sounds, the way a poem's flourishes may conceal its structure.

Collecting from the alleys is almost a secret activity; I'm nearly always alone with my dog, except for dogs penned in their yards and the occasional service truck. Each evening, however, we walk in a public park, where I nod to another gleaner. The man carries a plastic bag and a long stick with a curved and pointed end, briskly circling the park collecting aluminum cans. The stick allows him to snag cans from deep inside Dumpsters and from the ground with hardly a break in stride. Following him at slow Westie pace, I start lifting lids, usually closing them quickly on smelly trash and household garbage.

One day, I saw zipped plastic bags containing sheets, blankets, and comforters. As I stacked those on the sidewalk, Jerry went for the car. Next came folded clothing: sweat suits in bright colors; T-shirts from exotic places; several hats; a pile of sweaters with sequin designs. Finally, I hung into the depths to retrieve a box of souvenir salt and pepper shakers and a gallon tea jar.

After sorting out five sets of sheets and blankets that fit my beds, I hauled everything else to the thrift store. That night I dreamed of an elderly lady who beamed and patted my shoulder just as my grandmother might have.

Not long after, I opened the same trash can lid to find jumbled boxes containing an entire executive home office, including several expensive pen and pencil sets and engraved plaques for sports and sales achievements. Then came the packages of unopened supplies: envelopes in varied sizes, pens, staples, paper clips, highlighters, compasses, reams of paper, staplers, rulers, tape dispensers, correction fluid, paper punches, a paper cutter, leather-bound calendars, spiral-bound notebooks, stamp dispensers, a postal scale, and desk lamps. Still lower were whiskey glasses and bottles of whiskey and liqueurs, racks of well-smoked pipes, and boxes of tobacco.

And that wasn't all. When Jerry came back with the car, I was hefting shiny metal tool boxes with complete sets of expensive wrenches, followed by boxes of car polish and waxes. Since we seldom even wash our elderly vehicles, the automotive care items went to the thrift store, but we vastly supplemented our collections of tools, and I still haven't used up all the office supplies.

Jerry kept shaking his head and muttering, "To throw away tools." I think the story behind the collection might have involved a broken relationship and a woman's rage. I recall a time when I wanted to scour all trace of the offending male from my house, doing as much damage to his possessions as possible without going to jail. Empathizing, I left the engraved trophies, hoping she might tell him where she'd dumped his stuff.

The most spectacular item we've gleaned is an exercise machine dumped near the botanic garden. We prefer physical labor to mechanical exercise, so we walked past it for two days. Now it fits perfectly at the end of the couch in the sun porch, where I can exercise before my shower while watching the staff arrive at the school across the street every morning. And it's another perfect symbol of the intricate and sometimes puzzling benefits of gleaning. Physically, it's useful, but it also allows time for philosophical thinking and meditations on the way we conduct ourselves in this world.

Settled in my armchair, legs and arms tingling, I drink my second cup of coffee, eat homemade granola, and consider how we use our resources. My writing is mostly devoted to convincing people to be responsible, to curb our appetites, to make better choices. But I sometimes feel I am shouting across an immense abyss.

The word "gleaning" always calls up the same image: a painting I've seen only in cheap, faded prints in Sunday school classrooms in church basements. Jean Franççois Millet's 1857 painting *The Gleaners* depicts three women bending as they work in a grainfield. The women are laboriously picking up, stem by stem and kernel by kernel, grain that a hired harvest crew has dropped. A golden sunset makes beauty of the painstaking reaping, but the work was likely a practical necessity done to prevent starvation.

In sixteenth-century France, Millet's painting was a powerful, even risky, social comment because the poor were considered less than human—an ugly, dangerous tribe created only to work for the rich. Yet their right to scavenge fields was recognized and universally accepted. The concept has such power that several modern food banks incorporate "gleaning" into their names.

In modern times, of course, we might pity those poor, unsophisticated, uneducated peasants and donate money to good causes to help them. Or build taller, tighter fences around our fields to keep them out. Yet it's likely that they lived more mindful, efficient lives than we do, because gleaning—recycling—was a necessity, not something they had to train themselves to practice. They didn't learn their ways from public education campaigns about recycling. These were the folks, after all, who created pot-au-feu as the ultimate collection of leftovers. Now found among the most gourmet of recipes, the stew originated with a pot left simmering for days on the back of a stove. Peasants who worked for the rich often brought home leftover scraps of meat to create a richer broth, but the stew might contain anything edible a family could find.

Gleaning has always been part of my life, though I was slow to understand that it's a philosophy in addition to a method. Perhaps because I first saw Millet's painting in church, I have always thought of gleaning as being something more than scavenging or saving money. In some way, it's linked in my mind with an ethical duty—though that sounds suddenly too pompous for what I mean. As an example, I never have much spare cash, but gleaning allows me to contribute thousands of dollars' worth of usable goods to charities.

Gleaning is so much a part of my life now that it's a discipline, a doctrine. I must pay attention all the time, knowing today's discoveries may be physical objects, or the way a burst of light shines on a leaf.

Consider the complexity surrounding that oxygen bottle in our living room. Jerry's sister Susan lived a fast-paced corporate life before she fell in love with a mountain-climbing guide, but once she decided on her goals, she persisted against all challenges and trained herself with incredible fortitude. On her first trip up Everest, she was forced to turn back a few hundred yards short of the summit.

But she did it again: all the training, all the discipline. Furthermore, she might have left the scarred orange bottle that helped her breathe on that journey to be refilled and reused. Instead, she gave it to her brother, who encouraged and laughed with her; it has become a symbol, reminding us every day of her determination.

And there's more to this gleaning story. Climbing Everest has become popular as technology has improved, but getting up and down alive is so physically grueling that everything extra is abandoned by climbers descending. Retrieving the bodies of dead climbers is even too dangerous. So the sacred mountain was littered with garbage, particularly oxygen bottles, until Sherpas were paid for every oxygen bottle brought down the mountain. By 2002, the mountain was clean of bottles as high as Camp IV at twenty-six thousand feet. Nowadays, bottles from Everest climbs are auctioned on eBay. So, as is the case with many success stories, money plays a part.

As ranchers, my family didn't raise much of the grain I associate with literal gleaning. Instead, our cattle grazed on native grass provided by nature, sustaining themselves just as wild animals have for millennia. My father didn't teach me about ranching but demonstrated how to do it by the way he worked and lived. Our job, as I came to understand it, was to help the cattle survive while disturbing the landscape and wildlife as little as possible. His attitude made clear to me that we pursued our profession by fitting ranching into the structure nature had created around us— not by bulldozing the countryside into a shape that fit our needs and whims.

When I was learning to harvest hay from the alfalfa fields, my father told me to leave a wide strip unmown next to the fences. The tall grass provided both concealment for predators like coyotes and food for rabbits, deer, and other wildlife that might be their prey. "If we're so hard up we have to cut every blade of grass," he said, "it wouldn't save us anyway." Patiently, he practiced tending to our tools and machines, and equally to the country where we lived.

Our lives revolved around mindful use of what we had. By today's standards, we lived a frugal life. We raised cows and chickens, kept a garden, and ground grain bought from the neighbors to make our own bread. I hated wearing the secondhand clothes my mother bought me, especially in high school. If I'd been asked to explain then what was most important in my parents' lives, I might have quoted my father's dictum, "Never spend any money."

Though I was an adult when I first became aware of the word "recycling," we always practiced it. Even when I was most frustrated with the nit-picking in my parents' lectures, I knew that "waste not, want not" meant more than not squandering money or material goods. I sensed a subliminal clause with a broader meaning, requiring something more comprehensive from me.

Thirty years ago, when I moved back to the family ranch with my second husband, I kept hens for meat and eggs, feeding them vegetable peelings and the neighbors' grain. They roamed a large, fenced yard in front of their tiny, insulated house near my garden and ate trimmings from the vegetables I harvested.

One day, leaving the supermarket parking lot, I realized one Dumpster was overflowing with wrapped heads of lettuce. I slammed on the brakes, filled my pickup bed, drove home, piled the excess lettuce outside the chicken yard, and fed the ladies a head of lettuce a day for weeks.

Every time I went to town after that, I passed the trash bins after shopping and collected discarded lettuce, radishes, turnips, potatoes. My clucking chickens gathered at the gate when they saw my pickup, and their egg yolks turned a rich yellow.

Once, a store clerk dumping bottles of salad dressing questioned me, but when I explained that I was feeding my chickens on waste he shrugged and went back inside.

After Mother's Day, I filled the pickup with discarded carnations and enlisted a friend to ride in back of the truck flinging flowers as I drove down the street, tossing them into open car windows at stoplights. We detoured to the poorest part of town and handed a fistful of carnations to every woman we saw.

Then one day I pulled up to my Dumpster and saw a clerk standing on a ladder beside it, stabbing the packaged heads of lettuce with a long knife and pouring bleach over them.

"Why are you doing that?" I asked, perhaps a little hysterically.

"Management says people have been taking this stuff out and eating it, and they're afraid somebody will get sick and sue us," he said.

I suggested that people hungry enough to eat out of Dumpsters probably didn't have the number of an attorney at their fingertips, but he wasn't the manager, and he was, as he reminded me, "just doing his job."

When I got home, I called my extension agent. Bleach wouldn't hurt the chickens, he said; in fact, it ought to eliminate stomach parasites.

I kept collecting vegetables, but I also wrote letters to the store's management, urging them to donate the food to the shelters and other good causes in town. Eventually, the trash containers were empty of vegetables when I made my rounds, so perhaps my chickens helped change wasteful policies. I tried to explain this to the chickens, but they couldn't keep their minds on my speech. They kept eying the grass in their pen and snatching grasshoppers. Gleaning.

Living means gleaning; it means paying attention to whatever is around me at this moment. Mac still runs around enthusiastically, gleaning everything he can from his life. And I do my best, too. At a reading or speech, when a crowd has just applauded something I've written, I love to add, "By the way, I just want to tell you that everything I'm wearing is secondhand. And guess what I found in the alley last week?"

Something old, but perhaps the start of something new.

Intimmensity

ELIZA MURPHY

A born wanderer, Eliza Murphy tests her staying power a few blocks from the Willamette River, in Portland, Oregon. She contributes stories and reviews to *High Country News, Raw Vision,* and *Rain Taxi Review of Books.* Stained paper, broken bits, bones, rust, and ragged cloth found on the ground or waving from branches make their way into her pockets for later use in assemblages. During her circuitous journeys on foot, by bicycle, or behind the wheel of her car, she gathers stories about the tragic interface between wildlife and roads. Here, she writes about the confluence of the intimate and the immense—intimmensity.

Wings fanned out on sand, eyes missing, the bird's feathers stirred slightly as wind swept off the water and up the shore. Another dead bird lay wedged between the bones of old-growth forests on the beach at Cape Blanco. I wandered toward the mouth of the Elk River, a meandering walk punctuated by frequent detours to look at each dead bird I found. By the time I got to the river, I had counted thirteen.

Here, at the farthest western point in the continental United States, I felt like I was teetering on the edge of the world. I spotted all sorts of things deposited by the receding tide—sea weed, driftwood, stones, a few pieces of broken sand dollars, empty mussel shells.

There was also a lot of plastic confetti. This is the raw form of plastic—the pellets headed for melting, injecting, molding, and other methods of transformation, into the array of items in my medicine chest—caps for toothpaste, lotions, and potions; vitamin bottles; deodorant sticks, and samples of beauty products. While it looked wrong sprinkled in such a wild place, this stuff is ubiquitous. Great quantities of it drift on currents around the planet. This is the stuff that enters bird beaks, gets drawn into the mouths of fish and turtles, and slides down gullets, filling guts and blocking bodily exits. Some gets mistaken for food; other bits pepper a meal with this accidental condiment. Bellies fill with indigestible chaff, some of it also toxic, fooling birds into feeling full. No longer hungry, they quit eating. Some starve, others die of dehydration.

The carcasses wash up with discarded flip flops, spent inhalers, tampon applicators, fragments of wading pools that must have sprung leaks, bathtub toys, and cigar filters on beaches around the world.

Way out in the middle of the Pacific Ocean, well off the California coast, is a churning mass of plastic known as the North Pacific subtropical gyre. Estimated to be twice as large as the state of Texas, this vortex of anthropogenic debris swirls round and round in a tumbler of salt water, which breaks some larger debris into fragments, dulling the lurid colors but never breaking it down into its raw material—the liquid remains of prehistoric creatures that we fight wars over. Scientists estimate that it would take more than five hundred years for the plastic circulating currently to break down.

Floating refuse caught the attention of Captain Charles Moore while he was racing his boat *Alguita* across the Pacific. Seeing miles of bright objects floating in the water prompted him to devote his energy to investigating the extent of the problem, and to identify and confront the primary source of the deadly pollution. Moore made the mind-boggling and heartwrenching discovery that in the middle of the gyre mentioned above, plastic outweighs plankton six to one.

Four-fifths of the stuff originates on the land. The rest comes from cargo containers that fall overboard as ships list in high seas and trash gets tossed illegally off boats as a way to avoid disposal fees. That accounts for the debris that gets broken down into smaller particles. The other, even more deadly, plastic is easier to overlook as you beachcomb, unless you're sitting on your butt raking through sand with your fingers.

Some of the junk escapes the gyres (there are several of these in different locations) to drift on currents around the world, only to become marooned briefly somewhere on the planet, as far away as Antarctica. Some of the stuff Moore dredged out of this marine dump had been getting tumbled by the sea for over fifty years.

While sitting on the beach, I picked up handfuls of sand and let it sift through my fingers. I was left with little chips of plastic and opaque pellets that made me think of candy dots, only they had no color and I wasn't particularly inclined to pop them into my mouth.

Those tiny little pellets, plastic discs the size and shape of flattened, unsprouted mung beans, are known as "nurdles" or "mermaid tears." These are the building blocks of all those plastic things we use on a regular basis and take for granted: ChapStick tubes, toothbrushes, pens, beverage containers, as well as superfluous things used for fun: beach balls, lawn chairs, plastic flamingos, and Frisbees.

Calling these slippery things "mermaid tears" offends me. First off, it renders these "poison pills," as Moore calls them, innocuous, which they are not. Not only do these dreadful little buggers clog the digestive systems of sea creatures, they're also jam-packed with pollutants. Acting like sponges, they soak up all sorts of contaminants that wend their way to the sea from agricultural fields, effluent pipes, and storm drains—some have levels of polychlorinated biphenyls (PCBs) at concentrations of over one million times that of the water that carries them afloat for decades.

Mermaids cry real, salty tears. I am certain that their tears are made from their watery home, and once shed, they flow safely back into it.

Before turning in for the night, I walked at an angle into the drizzle-filled wind that battered everything that it touched. I stood with my hands buried in my raincoat pockets on the top of the bluff, listening and shivering as I heard those driftwood logs clanking against one another. Two hundred feet up and the percussion section played by the Pacific trembled up through my feet. I could feel things down to my bones. I couldn't stop thinking about those birds, the ground up bits of plastic.

Sleep eluded me. I stayed awake listening to what sounded like rifle shot ringing up the bluff and moving inland. Twenty-five-foot swells pounded the land below where I laid my head in a tiny cabin, named "Osprey," rented from the Oregon State Park. Eventually, I succumbed to Morpheus.

A dazzling, enchanted realm awaited me in the morning. Beads of light dangled from branches and clung to weeds. Overnight, the storm had dissipated, leaving behind a sky scrubbed clean of clouds. As dictated by the rules of staying in this rustic cabin, I made coffee on a camp stove outside. Tiny puffs of mist threaded through the tall ferns growing nearby. After drinking a sufficient amount of coffee, I headed back down the hill to the beach and wound around the rearranged logs, their lower halves dark as chocolate from soaking in water.

Delighted to feel a tad of warmth from the unexpected, welcome sunshine on a winter's day, I reveled in the break in the weather while I could. No one else was on the beach—no off-road vehicles had arrived yet to darken my mood.

As it turned out, I didn't need them for my mood to start spiraling downward. The dead birds that had captured my attention the day before had been drawn back into the sea. In their place were cracked bleach jugs, a banged-up gas can, chunks of Day-Glo Styrofoam floats crusted with live mussels, drinking straws, dish detergent, and beverage bottles. Lots of them, all of them new arrivals. And lots more fragments in sinuous bands extending down the beach.

I started filling my pockets. After my front pockets filled, I filled my back pockets. Then I bent my arm and jammed the crook with gritty, slimy junk. Then I folded onto the wet sand. I emptied my pockets and looked at the pile of garish trash in front of me. In my mind's eye I saw a bird gasp, choke, seize with a final breath, and drop from the sky. I could even see the spray of prismatic drops as it landed in the water.

My hands started to make a pair of wings. I wound plastic around plastic to form a body, attached bits of polyester fabric to rigid strips and a spent cap gun cartridge to make spread wings, using fishing line to keep everything in place. The first I'd make in homage to the birds that starve to death after ingesting plastic, this magical talisman inspired a plan to make an entire installation out of garbage gleaned from the beach. I've been calling it the *Plastic Sea*. I detest the sound of it, but I calls it as I sees it.

We have effectively reconstituted the oceans by enjoying the convenience of take-out food, by preventing pregnancy by pushing a pill a day out of a hard plastic case, or by catching a breath with a squirt of chemicals through a mouthpiece that disperses the medicine into passageways that lead to the lungs.

As the bird takes shape, I consider the *Plastic Sea*. It sounds a bit like "plasticity." I give it a different sound—the "c" is hard, making it rhyme with "rickety." Icky "Plastickity." Or "plasti city," those centers where steam emerges from towers that reach way into the sky, smokestacks that manufacture storms. The towers projecting from factories where pellets get melted and made into goods that ride the conveyor belts to get shut inside boxes, to be carried away in an endless stream. A stream of want.

Every month or so I make a trek out to the Oregon coast to collect more plastic. I bring it home and dump it on my dining room floor and use it to fashion the sad collection of artifacts gathering at the

A mermaid with Styrofoam bosoms takes shape. Her kinky hair is made from unraveled plastic rope; her tail is netting chock-full of bits of debris—some of it recognizable, some of it of mysterious origin. Photo courtesy of Eliza Murphy.

18

edge of the room. A mermaid with Styrofoam bosoms takes shape. Her kinky hair is made from unraveled plastic rope; her tail is netting chock-full of bits of debris—some of it recognizable, some of it of mysterious origin. Last week I started to make a salmon. Steeped in chemicals that mimic hormones, the pellets they swallow disrupt their reproductive processes.

I am building a mock natural history DIE-O-RAMA. For a backdrop, I'll paint a seascape on sheets I'll buy by the pound from the Goodwill bins around the corner from where I live in southeastern Portland. Most likely, I'll have to sew a few together because I want the cloth to spill onto the floor to mimic waves— blue and green bits will become a sewn-on crest, with white plastic on the edge to imitate foam. Mutant birds will fill the foreground, and a few will hang from the ceiling, as if those makeshift wings could launch one of them into the air.

But is this effort superfluous? Not enough, yet too much at the same time? What possible difference can I make by gathering debris from a place where there will always be more to replace what I remove? I think of Sisyphus rolling that damn ball up the hill. Tide rolls in every twelve hours, carrying havoc in primary colors, garish hues. Will I find a gallery owner willing to give space for this installation? Will anyone who views it find more than food for thought? Am I veering into perilous territory by asking art to expand consciousness, to offer something to the viewer other than relief from the banal workaday world through visual language?

I have to talk back, though. I'd be going against my nature if I didn't put in my two cents' worth. To contribute something to the vital conversation about the fate of all life on this astonishing planet we are collectively killing off. At an accelerated pace.

The birds that keep me company in my dining room, destined for a more public place—they are a form of offering. I took dead stuff to give it new life.

A few weeks ago, my head filled with dire predictions about the local effects of climate change, I felt guilty for driving my Camry two hundred miles round-trip to reach Cape Disappointment, a point around the bend from the mouth of the Columbia River. A deep longing for salt air, negative ions, ozone, spaciousness, or whatever it is that keeps me returning to the sea to rejuvenate had held me in its grip for weeks. I was irritable for having spent weeks inside buildings, cornered by right angles and recirculated air. I could not go another day without wandering surfaces that yielded to my weight.

My problems contract when I'm confronted by the ocean's appearance of limitlessness. Even though I know that the ocean is finite, the illusory effect of infinity helps rearrange my priorities. By playing with my sense of scale, the ocean makes my personal grievances shrink in scope. But the symptoms of its worsening ailments—bird carcasses, plastic confetti—demand that I heed the warnings. Back home, every plastic bag gets washed and rewashed until the sides rip. I buy as much as I can in bulk.

I went to the beach with mixed feelings, a deep and uneasy ambivalence churning in my gut. The day before my decision to make the trek out to the coast I had run out of materials for my installation. On one hand, I wanted to find a beach clean of debris— sparkling in the sunlight with only seaweeds and driftwood strewn on the dark sand and plenty of birds running to escape a wave or just clearing the water's surface. On the other hand, I went not only to refuel my spirit by feeling salt air on my skin, but to find more stuff.

Deep ruts ran up the beach. Strangers waved from jeeps and trucks as they raced north or south. Near the ruts, shiny beer cans glinted and Slim Jim wrappers shuddered in the breeze. This was not the refuse I had come to collect. I was after the stuff that the sea had altered, the stuff that had returned from a voyage.

It didn't take long before I filled my bags. I got more selective in what I picked up, opting to skip the tug-of-war that comes with yanking on buried rope. I chose blue over orange, stuck to items no bigger than twice the size of my fist. There was no way I could remove all of it. Wishing for a dearth of the stuff, I found a plethora instead. Rope, bottle tops, and beverage bottles were the most common items I found. Among the debris, I scored a mold for a mother dolphin and her offspring. Nothing but the essentials. Next time I'll bring a large garbage bag just for the bottles.

Someone had scrawled in the sand: GARBAGE.

I paused there, knowing at least one other kindred spirit had passed this way since high tide.

This interface between land and sea reveal symptoms that point to a syndrome, a complex ailment. Like the netting I unearthed with the toe of my shoe, something I see as a physical demonstration of the invisible matrix underlying all things, linking everything to everything else on the planet, in the cosmos—to me, this bit of webbing is a symbol of our interconnectedness. What goes around.

Tiny barnacles cling to the strands of black mesh. The sea's surface resembles netting—a harlequin pattern distorted by perpetual movement, the lacing of lines on the palm of my hand, cross-hatchings in sand left by overlapping waves. Branching patterns. There are so many clues in the patterns surrounding us.

Pull on one strand of that web, the rest has to flux, adapting to the shift. The dead birds are related to climate change. We *Homo sapiens* initiated and now help accelerate global warming.

"We have met the enemy," Pogo declared, "and he is us."

I am no scientist, but I pay attention. My imagination works in a way I call "intimmensity." I can probably credit Dr. Suess for my fascination with infinity, later Blake for his overwrought grain of sand. From my experience, starting with the intimate, moving outward to view things more systemically, I can make connections. I'm sure there are plenty of experts to find fault with my leapfrogging. But stories in the news tell me my speculations are not so far-fetched.

I guess it all goes back to those factories that comprise the plasti-city. Machines that use energy drum on and on, changing raw materials into pellets, the building blocks that get shipped to another factory where they get transformed into something else that'll find its way to a shelf then to yet another destination where it gets used or broken or becomes obsolete or goes out of style or gets separated from its lid. Then it gets hauled somewhere. More fuel consumption, more carbon dioxide pumped into the atmosphere. It arrives at a landfill. Leaves shore on a barge. Gets hurled from the back of a pickup truck into a ditch in an out-of-the-way place. Somewhere out of sight.

Until it gets a lift in a current of water. And finds its way to the sea. Where an albatross catches it, after flying hundreds of miles for food for her hatchling. She returns to the nest to regurgitate the nodule of plastic with its scant plankton into the eager mouth, open to receive her bounty. Only the cigar filter doesn't fit quite right. Neither does the glow-in-the-dark sea star. Choke. Gasp.

Whether wrapped around feet, lodged in a windpipe, fattening a belly, or poisoning the bloodstream, the byproducts of our wants are wiping out the animals. The colossal dimensions of a tiny pellet.

Blacktop Cuisine

MICHAEL ENGELHARD

Michael Engelhard commutes between the Colorado Plateau and Alaska, where he works as a wilderness guide. The editor of two anthologies and author of *Where the Rain Children Sleep* and *Wild Moments*—a collection of encounters with unmangled fauna—he has contributed to *Outside, Utne Reader, San Francisco Chronicle, Canoe & Kayak, Arizona Highways,* and other magazines. Trained as an anthropologist, Engelhard knows how to keep a straight face while partaking of exotic foods.

"Dinner is ready, guys." We pull our chairs to the kitchen table, as Bart takes a bubbling casserole from the oven. The fragrance of masa, chilies, and cilantro fills the room.

"Looks great," I say, forking up my first bite. The meat is a bit stringy, with a gamey tang to it. "What is it?"

"Bobcat tamales," Bart says. Furry white eyebrows wiggle up his forehead like caterpillars, accentuating the trademark Blankenship grin.

"Where did you get it, Bart?"

Only Native Americans with religious permits are allowed to possess eagle feathers.

"Oh, outside of Pagosa. At first I thought it was a standard poodle."

"Hmmm . . . interesting," I say, taking another, more tentative bite. Not what I imagined cat to taste like. And not "like chicken" at all.

My friend and roommate Bart is a latter-day mountain man. He works for Outward Bound and sometimes for an outdoors survival school. With his ex-wife, he authored a book about flint knapping and other Stone Age skills. His chert and bottle glass arrowheads are not just functional—they are works of art. He has taught his children to catch trout with bare hands and knows how to weave fishing nets from home-processed yucca fibers. Bart's idea of dressing up for a night on the town is to don his brain-tanned buckskin shirt and pants. I never know what will show up in our freezer from day to day.

Like other aficionados, Bart became a road kill gourmet by default. As the founder of a school for primitive skills, he needed furs, hides, feathers, antlers, and sinew in order to teach tanning, arrow fletching, or tool hafting. Highways seemed like the best places to procure these materials. Bart started by calling the Colorado Department of Transportation for recent deer kills, and there were usually a few in the Boulder vicinity. Skinning the carcasses, Bart found that much of the meat was still good. Generally, he is not too concerned about ticks, rabies, or tularemia. He washes his hands and any meat thoroughly and otherwise thinks that a dose of bacteria will keep his immune system strong. When in doubt, he has a surefire way of testing road kill. "I cook a small piece without seasoning and taste it. If it tastes like it was dipped in vinegar then it likely won't make you sick."

As a parent of two, with little income, Bart is quick to point out the economic advantage of eating road kill. Since the 1980s, he has supplemented his family's larder with deer, elk, and bobcat. At times, up to a third of the meat consumed by the Blankenships comes from fender benders. At thirty to fifty pounds of usable meat per deer and a store value of two to five dollars a pound, the savings can be substantial. But unlike some of my dirtbag river guide friends, Bart draws the line at Dumpster diving, which he considers gross.

A roster of Bart's "trophies" reads like a Who's Who of western wildlife. My friend admits to having boiled and eaten a great horned owl once. "I ran it over and felt I had to do something with it," he says. But generally, the "exotics"—coyote, raccoon, fox, opossum, wild hog, otter, badger, and mink—are set aside to be made into mittens or arrow quivers.

The legalities (and reality) of peeling bunnies off the asphalt can be Byzantine. While Bart dodges traffic to avoid suffering his dinner's fate, he does well to remember federal and state laws. It is illegal, for example, to collect certain animals, from the road or elsewhere. Only Native Americans with religious permits are allowed to possess eagle feathers. The state of Utah issues a permit each time an individual wants to retrieve a killed animal. And while motorists in Arizona are entitled to keep meat from a deer they have hit, the same act can land you in prison in Oregon. On long road trips, scrounging can become quite an ordeal. Bart remembers one outing in particular. "We were driving in Kansas and had four raccoons in bags tied to the roof, and they were thawing, and blood was dripping down the windows. We found we weren't allowed to have them in Kansas, even though we picked them up elsewhere. So we ended up beating it back to Colorado where they'd be legal." Another time, Bart's youngest son threw up in his car seat, sickened by half a fox his Dad was transporting. On the bright side, the mess got them out of a citation for speeding.

Even at his home, the Law keeps an eye on Bart's preparations. He recalls the time a concerned neighbor alerted the authorities. "The EPA came and asked where our toxic chemicals were for tanning the hides. When we showed them the buckets of brains, they said we might want to keep a lid on to keep out the flies. The Department of Wildlife came while we were using a ceiling fan to dry some furs; but they left with a brochure of our primitive skills school. The fire department came when we smoked hides but went away when they saw the smoke coming out of our woodstove and going straight into a deer hide. The City of Boulder came and left, and so did the police."

While Bart may strike some people as eccentric or a throwback to fur rendezvous times, more and more Americans are discovering the potential of road kill. Taxidermists fix flattened pelts for natural history museum exhibits. A gallery owner in South Dakota plucks porcupine quills to fashion into jewelry. A New Mexico sculptor and tattoo artist assembles bones into motorcycles or "Gnarleys." An Arizona state biologist prepares skulls and other skeletal parts to be used as educational kits in schools. Frozen corpses serve him as models for scientific illustrations; fresher meat ends up on the barbecue grill or as food for his boas and pythons.

For all their entertainment value and utility, creative uses of road kill can hardly disguise the social and ecological costs incurred daily on U.S. highways. Aside from abetting habitat fragmentation, pollution, and noise, roads take a more direct and bloody toll on biodiversity. Vehicles kill hundreds of millions of animals every year. Snakes and amphibians—including many endangered species— take the brunt of this onslaught. Not even our national parks are safe. On Yellowstone's roads alone, 1,559 large mammals died between 1989 and 2003. To wit, the boundary between victims and perpetrators becomes blurred. Two hundred people died last year in about 250,000 collisions with animals. The average repair of an automobile damaged by deer (or more specifically, by reckless driving) runs around two thousand dollars.

Perhaps, like our fellow creatures, we humans are not hard-wired for life in the fast lane. Neither, some critics insist, were we meant to eat carrion.

It's true that the thought of consuming possum paella or rattle-snake ragout will induce dry heaves in most people. Yet the wide-spread prejudice against scavenging only masks humble origins. It is a credo, a pretense akin to the convert's denial of obsolete pagan practices. The rank reality may disgust many: gleaning is in our genes. It helped us become who we are.

The concept of Man the Hunter (and by extension Woman the Gatherer) is not entirely the product of gender biases ruling science or politics. It also appears as a case of myth making by a species in search of dignity, a species still largely intent on seeing itself as the apex of—if not separated from—the animal kingdom. *Nature* is red in tooth and claw; *we* are the paragons of table manners and fancy cooking. In truth, rather than wielding spears and skewering woolly mammoths, *Homo sapiens* began its career as a beggar in Nature's soup kitchen. In an eat-or-be-eaten world, bone picking proved to be more efficient than gathering (especially when protein yield is compared), yet less risky than hunting—an optimal foraging strategy. Opportunists to the bone, our hominid ancestors on the African savanna filled their bellies with scraps wrangled from lion or leopard kills, in competition with hyenas, jackals, and vultures. In this scenario, the invention of stone tools later gave us an edge over other scavengers by facilitating dismemberment, as well as marrow and brain extraction (which can be tough with fingernails and underdeveloped dentition). Speech and cooperation followed suit, in turn giving birth to more complex behaviors like big game hunting and presidential campaigning.

Supposedly, anthropology can even shed light on the foul reputation of blacktop cuisine. Evolutionary psychologists speculate that our revulsion at eating dead and rotten things (as opposed to just rotten things, like Limburger cheese) developed as an adaptive trait. This sort of "intuitive microbiology" helped early *Homo* to avoid lethal cases of food poisoning. Physical anthropologists, on the other hand, like to point out that, even under an equatorial sun, it can take up to forty-eight hours for flesh to begin to putrefy. Furthermore, carcasses produced by "natural" death are likely to be free of dangerous parasites, because most such deaths result from malnutrition rather than from disease. Good news for the harvesters of ditches and interstates, I guess.

In my home state, Alaska, the road kill menu is less varied than Bart's backyard fare. As if to compensate, everything is super-sized here, including the servings. (An adult 1,100-pound moose normally yields about 700 pounds of meat, meat that is much leaner and more nutritious than beef.) Trains and vehicles annihilate about 820 moose per annum, carnage only surpassed in Sweden, where motorists cull moose populations by 4,000 to 6,000 animals each year. About 120 Alaskan moose annually fall prey to the Alaska Railroad's yellow-and-blue engines. With a sense of humor honed at fifty degrees below zero, residents of this state call the train between Fairbanks and Anchorage "the Moose Butcher." When northern lights play above snowdrifts, animals follow the plowed tracks as substitutes for easy trails. Allegedly, bull moose even take on locomotives—as they would rack-sporting competitors—during the fall rut. Heavy snowfalls and overcrowding can drive moose into urban areas, leading to an increase in fatalities. Occasionally, the quick stroke of technology also cuts short the lives of black bears, Dall's sheep, and mountain goats. Sixteen-hour nights and icy roads result in tons of high-quality foodstuff: prime cuts, tenderloin, spareribs, and minced meat. And at subarctic temperatures, this bonanza does not spoil easily.

Alaska's urban and semi-urban centers have therefore implemented programs to retrieve and distribute road kill to the needy. In Anchorage, Fairbanks, and the Matanuska-Susitna Valley, and on the Kenai Peninsula, hundreds of charities and individuals benefit from poor visibility, speeding, drunk driving, and poor road conditions. Nearly all road kill moose in the state goes to nonprofit organizations, many of which are churches. Beneficiaries must respond within thirty minutes to a coordinator's call to salvage the meat. If they fail to do so, the follower-up on a list will be given a chance. Alaska Fish and Game biologists or hunters affiliated with the nonprofits often are called upon to shoot wildlife injured in accidents.

Eileen Brooks is the road kill coordinator for the Anchorage region and Mat-Su Borough of south-central Alaska. Colleagues refer to her as "Queen of the Gut Pile." But according to Eileen, the Blankenship diet helps alleviate hardship in a place where the cost of living is high. "A lot of people can't afford to buy steaks or even hamburger," she says. And while many Alaskans enjoy the fruits of subsistence hunting and fishing, that venue is barred to the urban poor. In Eileen's area alone, one hundred nonprofits are signed up for road kill in a typical winter, and some community churches receive an average of ten moose a year.

A major tenet of sustainable living admonishes us not simply to recycle but rather to curb wastefulness in the first place. Unfortunately, a society obsessed with driving is unlikely to ever fully embrace measures that reduce wildlife mortality on its roads. Speed limits, better signage, fencing, or animal crosswalks all could prevent unnecessary deaths. Tight budgets and narrow minds, however, ensure that ecological attrition will continue. Short of all-out solutions, we can at least honor the casualties with a token gesture. Sharing the mangled flesh in a form of unholy communion, we acknowledge their sacrifice.

So, let us show some respect. Let us break the mold of culinary routine. To connoisseurs tired of French, Thai, or Mexican, Bart recommends the chef's special: grille gopher in crankcase oil, with a side of creamed coyote—guaranteed to tickle the palate while sparing the wallet. (Do yourselves a favor though, and skip the muskrat mush.)

Bon appétit!

Gleaning for Lillie

LAURA PASKUS

Laura Paskus is a writer living in Albuquerque. She has written for *High Country News, Orion, Audubon Magazine,* and the *Santa Fe Reporter,* and often focuses on environmental issues in the Southwest. Although she was raised on the East Coast, no place has ever felt like home to her save the high desert of New Mexico. She's grateful for the privilege of being a reporter whose job it is to ask lawmakers and bureaucrats questions that might make them uncomfortable. But most of all she's proud that her daughter, Lillie Jane, is a New Mexico native who makes environmental reporting a worthwhile pursuit, and who from an early age developed a respect for cactus and an affinity for noisy grackles.

My husband, Hollis, and I are at the flea market with other roving diehards. Even though it's three days before Christmas—and the flea market, according to my husband, is the perfect place to holiday shop—freezing temperatures are apparently keeping the crowds at bay. Framing Albuquerque's east side, the Sandia Mountains are just beginning to allow the sun to stretch across the parking lot of the New Mexico State Fairgrounds, where patches of snow still linger in the shade. A few frozen puddles have been shattered, their ice too great a temptation for snow-starved Albuquerque kids.

As we watch a woman struggle to load her son—wrapped burrito-like in polyester blankets—into a wagon, Hollis rubs his hands together, pulls his knit hat over his ears, and hits the flea market. Our daughter, Lillie, is off with her grandmother this morning, and we're free to cruise the flea market at our leisure in the freezing cold. Without her, it feels like we're on a date, and I'm a little giddy to be hanging out with my husband, just the two of us.

We stroll past every imaginable object for sale: kiddie wagons, car parts, tools, candlesticks, dishes, rugs, stereo equipment, books, records, clocks, strollers, photographs and framed prints, DVDs and videos, clothes and hats, knickknacks and bric-a-brac, furniture, tires, lampshades. Lingering at the tailgate of one truck is a roving crowd of men—it's the only place busy this morning. As we move closer, I see buckets full of power tools. We peer but keep moving.

Suddenly, we're moving very fast: "That's them!" Hollis points to two young hipster guys holding records under their arms. They're his main competition for snatching up piles of fifty-cent and one-dollar records—everything from Robert Frost reading his poetry to Herbie Mann and Sonny Rollins, Aretha Franklin and Ray Charles, even War and Black Sabbath. He grabs my arm and makes me tail them for a few blocks at the market. Ever the hunter, he's studying his prey, determined to learn their patterns, determined to prevent them from scoring the records he wants.

I've got to give it to him: the man can shop. Six years ago, when we first started dating, he came home bearing a frilly white blouse from a secondhand store. ("You love pirates!" he'd said.) There was also the maroon and beige checked sleeveless jumpsuit with a gold anchor belt buckle he brought home to me soon after we'd moved in with one another. ("You can wear this when we have a dinner party!") During those heady honeymoon days, he also hauled home a mosaic-topped coffee table with a gold atomic pattern

We stroll past every imaginable object for sale: kiddie wagons, car parts, tools, candlesticks, dishes, rugs, stereo equipment, books, records, clocks, strollers.

in the center, a double-decker macramé plant hanger with a built-in light, a metal schoolteacher's desk, a six-foot-long green couch in perfect condition, and a Japanese style wardrobe screen. One birthday he even surprised me with a 1964 Oldsmobile Dynamic. ("Happy birthday, babe!") The brakes were fickle, the radiator hissed, the shocks were nonexistent, and the gas tank required lead additive. But for a few months, I was the envy of all the young men in town.

"Goodwill is too commercial, consignment shops are too expensive," he'd once told me, "and everyone knows to go to the Salvation Army." He hunts and fishes, and apparently his brain is wired not only to find the stretch of trout stream where no one else will bother him but to sniff out the best estate sales, hole-in-the-wall shops, and small-town secondhand stores full of old-time dresses and farm equipment. And God forbid you drive through Florida with the man, as I did on our honeymoon. We did U-turn after U-turn as he spotted secondhand stores en route to Key West. Florida, of course, with its frequently thinned senior population, is a thrifter's dream.

To be sure, there have been some lemons, most notably the seven-foot-tall wooden cabinet we brought home to use as a pantry. Infested with moths, we spent more than a year slapping those fluttery bastards and trying to bug proof our dried goods before finally abandoning to the carport what had seemed like such a sweet score.

In fact, looking around our house, it's shocking to take note of what was someone else's before it was ours. It would not be an exaggeration to say that most of our stuff has been gleaned from elsewhere, plucked from the desert, lugged off the side of the road, and snatched from under the grasp of other bargain hunters. The majority of our books are secondhand, as is our furniture and the music we listen to (on a secondhand record player). On the shelves—in lieu of vases and ceramic knickknacks—are animal skulls, bighorn sheep horns, rocks, shells, a gourd from the garden, and miscellaneous animal parts. Produce hangs in a wire basket from the flea market by the back door (which we hope to replace, by the way, with another door from the ReStore, which sells construction waste and secondhand building materials). A fair number of our plants are from cuttings we'd propagated, or else are plants my husband rescued from being plowed under during road construction. Out the front door, there's a view of the fence Hollis built with latillas from a salvage thinning project in the Cibola National Forest; out the back door is compost he's hauled from a stable up the road. Even the desk I'm writing at is from an estate sale. I often wonder about the person who sat here before me—and yes, I use the ruler I found inside one of the drawers, and we set aside the bonus box of matches near our woodstove.

Recently, we have delved into an entirely new realm of gleaning: Dumpster diving. Well, actually, that term isn't entirely accurate, since the food is from boxes next to the Dumpsters.

Here's the thing—and I'm leaving out some of the details in the interest of selfishly protecting our food source—our grocery store leaves its less-than-perfect produce outside. And when I say "less-than-perfect," I really mean just a tiny bit shy of perfect. Thanks to the irrational need Americans have for bananas sans brown spots, apples without divots, peaches without soft spots, potatoes without eyes, and garlic and onions without green shoots, tons and tons of food each day go to waste.

Two springs ago, Hollis was looking for supplemental greens for our chickens, which already eat our scraps, dig through the compost pile, and scratch for bugs in the yard. During a routine trip to the grocery store, he'd spotted boxes of produce left behind the store, next to the Dumpster. A chicken bonanza! They were able to dig through the piles, eating organic lettuce and bok choy, picking apart bunches of bananas, and having a chicken field day with apples and squash. After too many jokes about how our chickens were eating better than we were, we started peeking through those boxes before delivering them to the yappy hens and bossy rooster. A closer look revealed pounds and pounds of produce we could eat ourselves. From that point, the hunt was on.

Last summer, Hollis walked in with the proudest grin I'd seen since the pirate shirt days. He was carrying two cases of Palisade peaches from Colorado. Organic Palisade peaches from Colorado. Two cases of these babies. Some had bruises, a few were mushy, but they all were edible. We spent the afternoon and evening slicing, pitting, and bagging them for the freezer. I had seen these in the store earlier in the week for $1.99 per pound, looked at them longingly, then moved on. But for the next few months we ended up eating peach cobbler, peach salsa, peach sauce on fish, and peach juice; my infant daughter, Lillie, ate so many peaches that her butt was regularly stained orange throughout the summer and early fall.

(As an aside, we also buy produce from a local farm, where we are members of a community-supported agriculture project. In the same way that I take Lillie to that farm along the Rio Grande each pick-up day hoping she'll grow up favoring fruit over candy and always knowing where food really comes from, I also hope she'll grow up valuing thrift over waste.)

All of these ideas about gleaning were solidified for me one snowy afternoon after Christmas, when Hollis returned home toting two cases of produce. We rummaged around, separating our food from that for the chickens. In the end, we came out with one ear of corn, two Red Anjou pears, fifteen potatoes, eight apples, four white onions, six yellow bananas, one carrot, nine zucchinis, six squashes, one tomato, two kiwis, a colander full of not-quite-ripe plantains, six bags of lettuce, four heads of Live Gourmet butter lettuce (the ones with their roots still attached, in space-age plastic containers), and about ten oranges. For their part, the chickens got about twenty pounds of overripe bananas, oyster mushrooms, more lettuce, and a bunch of oranges.

We spent that snowy day chopping, cooking, and freezing: we sliced and froze French fry sticks and grated potatoes for latkes, made an enormous pot of calabacitas, cooked two helpings of apple crisp, and cooked and froze apple slices for fruit smoothies. As the snowstorm stretched on, our electricity went out for almost twenty-four hours, causing panic that our work would be in vain.

What's weird is that during that snowstorm—when all our neighbors were without electricity and unable to leave their homes—I was too embarrassed to share the oranges and bags of lettuce we couldn't eat. This happens a lot. Oftentimes, serving a delicious meal to guests, who exclaim over the tasty, fresh, organic produce, I find myself refraining from saying things like, "We got this food for free!" or "It's all from the trash, can you believe it?" And I definitely don't mention that the food our infant daughter is eating was almost trash, too.

And this is the funny thing: I'm embarrassed that we eat food instead of allowing it to be wasted? Shouldn't there be mass outrage that while many people don't have enough to eat, perfectly good food is chucked out the door each day? What's going on here?

When I ask the produce manager at our grocery store about their policy, she explains that anything marked or approaching funny-looking goes into a reduced-price bin. Anything wilting or moldy goes in boxes out next to the Dumpster. When I say that this makes me pretty sad, she waves me off, assuring me it's fine—"A lot gets bought," she keeps repeating. But a young guy standing behind her, stocking mushrooms, catches my eye and shakes his head.

And as egregious as that policy sounds, it's even worse in a place such as Wild Oats. They don't sell reduced-price produce. Instead, once produce starts even hinting at nappiness, it goes into a fifty-gallon drum and gets sent off to the landfill. When asked why we can't just take the scroff for our chickens, we get a mumbled response about the health department.

According to a 2006 study by the U.S. Department of Agriculture, New Mexico is ranked number two in the entire nation in terms of "food insecurity." That term appears to have come into use only recently and is defined by the state as "uncertain or limited access to enough food for an active, healthy life." In other words, it means you don't know from where your next meal is coming. Not only that, but according to a 2006 study by the New Mexico Association of Food Banks, 238,000 New Mexicans sought emergency food in 2005—an increase of 38 percent since 2001. (For comparison's sake, New Mexico's population in 2005 was about 1.9 million.) Meanwhile, perfectly good produce goes to waste every day. And for some reason, I'm the one feeling shameful.

As mothers are prone to doing, I'm hopeful that Lillie will grow into a strong, smart, and compassionate young woman and that she will have a worthwhile world to inherit. I'm also hopeful that she and her peers will see fit to overcome their parents' examples and to stop acting like idiots when it comes to a lot of things, including food, consumerism, and natural resources.

I want Lillie to grow up knowing that wearing secondhand clothing or playing with toys or books from the flea market isn't necessarily about saving your own money—though that's a nice benefit. It's about using what's already available. It's about paying attention, finding what you need, fixing it if you need to, and passing it on when you're done.

I also want her to grow up knowing that food is sacred. That there's more to the postconsumer lifespan of a banana than simply "eat or throw away." In our house, you eat it if it's edible, no matter the spots or the bruises. If something has progressed beyond edible, it goes to the chickens; if they don't want it, it goes into the compost pile to nourish next season's garden. In other words, food has no place in the trash.

Keeping food out of the trash serves a purpose beyond our own household, as well. Organic produce is expensive, in part at least because whenever some is wasted, the stuff that's still on the shelves must be sold at a high enough price to make up for that loss, thereby putting it out of the financial reach of many families. This perpetuates an ugly cycle that exposes more and more children to toxic chemicals. It comes down to this: I feed my child organic food because pesticides and nasty fertilizers have no place in her beautiful little body. Nor do they have a place in any child's body. By supporting organic growers, we can help cut down on the numbers of other babies—living next to fields with their parents who work there or even living downstream from agricultural areas—who are exposed to toxic chemicals. And that's why the waste of organic produce in particular really gets my goat.

So, actually, while I drone on and on about why it's a shame to waste, Lillie has more to teach me than I realize: she doesn't mind mushy bananas or soft pears. She derives great joy from pointing at the chickens in the backyard and playing with leaves. She's never been in an SUV or insisted on a bigger house. And she's the one, after all, who is so careful to fetch and eat each and every crumb that falls from her biscuit—she teaches me that the five-second rule is overly conservative and that there's absolutely nothing wrong with gleaning.

Good Circulation

JOHN CLAYTON

John Clayton (www.johnclaytonbooks.com) is the author of *The Cowboy Girl: The Life of Caroline Lockhart*. He lives in a small town in Montana. Recently, a house remodel filled his garage with potential garage-sale items just as winter was about to put an end to garage-sale season. Then one Saturday morning John watched a pickup truck ram into his Jeep and drive off—the third hit-and-run on his vehicles in a month. And so was born the Instant Garage Sale, a bargain hunter's dream. Two dollars for a TV, three dollars for the DVD player or a hefty table to put them on. Any offer accepted: "We've got to empty that garage before we're rendered immobile!"

At a friend's garage sale several years ago, I saw a copy of Ivan Doig's book *This House of Sky*. I bundled it with my other purchases, but when my friend went to ring it up, I said, "Jean, I'm not going to pay for this one."

"Why not?"

I opened the front cover and showed her my name written inside of it. "Because I loaned it to you two years ago!"

Our town is so small that I always expect encounters with previous owners of garage-sale items.

Our town is so small that I always expect encounters with previous owners of garage-sale items. "Oh, look!" someone might say. "You've got our toaster!" He'd have sold the toaster several years ago—perhaps even several garage sales ago—and it circulated around to me.

I understand that some people might find shame in such an encounter, but to me it is all part of a natural cycle. You benefit from a toaster until for some reason it has no benefit left for you. Then you pass it along to where someone else can gain additional benefits from it.

Such exchanges happen in the big city, too, but there you're not likely to re-encounter your appliances while visiting a friend. Here, when the couple who sold me my rice cooker comes over, they wax nostalgic about it. I offer to sell it back to them at twice the dollar I paid for it.

I became a garage-sale aficionado fifteen years ago when I was an impoverished young bachelor just arrived in town. I had no furniture. So I went to garage sales. During my first couple of weeks in town, I bought a couch, easy chairs, a bureau, a kitchen table, pots and pans, plates, glasses, and silverware. I bought sheets, blankets, and the mattress to put them on. I laid the mattress and sheets on the floor until later I bought a garage-sale bedframe.

Eventually, I started operating on both sides of the garage-sale equation. For example, when I first arrived, I bought lots of coffee tables. I just thought a living room needed them. Whenever I saw a used coffee table, I'd judge whether it was better than the one I had. If it was, I'd upgrade, and my discards went to garage sales, where I hoped they would entice some young, budding collector.

Likewise, I once decided I needed a waffle iron. I found one at a garage sale. But when I took it home, I didn't like the way it worked, and so I sent it off again. Then I bought another waffle iron, but I didn't like it either. (It wasn't the same one, was it? The thought just occurs to me now.)

I typically donated such items to cause-based sales, such as my town's annual Habitat for Humanity fund-raiser. Some people treat garage sales as personal fund-raisers, but to me it's more about the flow of useful goods, a sort of community recycling program.

There are some items, of course, that never fit in the program. I've never bought a toothbrush at a garage sale, or underwear. They're just too personal. Nor have I ever found a file cabinet or a dog toy. For some reason, those are both items that you absolutely hold onto until they completely fall apart.

Recently, I've gotten married, and, thanks to the combining of households, I've become a net garage-sale donor. For example, my wife bought me a new gas-powered barbecue grill, so I took my old one to Habitat for Humanity for its sale. The igniter is broken, and the lid is dribbled with roofing tar, but I attached a piece of masking tape announcing to prospective buyers: "Works!" I trust that it is now serving its purpose for someone at a different stage of life.

Our town is small enough that I may meet those folks some-day. I hope they haven't scraped off the roofing tar, because I'd like to recognize their grill. I could tell them some stories about it.

All That We Leave Behind

LAURA KATERS

Laura Katers has elaborate daydreams of being a minimalist. She spent the last two summers teaching environmental education in Australia and owes many laughs, and life lessons, to the students and people she met while there. Her work has appeared in *More Sand in My Bra: Funny Women Write from the Road, Again!* and *Backpacker Magazine,* as well as in several local newspapers and publications. She believes in the unifying force of humor and honesty, and that if we're going to do anything good for the planet in our lifetime, we're going to need a healthy supply of both.

The first time I saw a "bin" in Australia, I was confused. In several large cardboard boxes, there was a monstrous disarray of clothes: sweatshirts with holes, T-shirts with stains, jeans made in Asia and in a size so small I could barely squeeze an arm through one of the legs. There were socks, ripped backpacks, purses, sweater vests, belts, single shoes, sunglasses, and homemade T-shirts with spray-painted declarations—"I'm a big deal." This behemoth mound of crap puzzled me until I gazed along a bulging side of one of the boxes and landed on the words: "Take Me."

Standing in the back hallway of an old house reserved for international volunteers—with meager clothing worn so thin most pieces were transparent—I felt a tingle. I'd been teaching environmental education in South Australia, the coldest state, with a lingering sore throat and hacking cough. I'd prepared myself for kangaroos and eucalyptus leaves, but what I hadn't counted on was spending most nights frozen between the bedsheets and losing circulation in my extremities. Looking at the shirts and pants and everything else bursting from the television-sized boxes, I suddenly imagined myself waking up in an inferno, sweat-drenched and grinning.

"You've got to be shitting me," the words came out as barely a whisper.

There was only one problem. One of my students, Jen—who was with me—was the same size as I was; she was fast, strong, and also in dire need of warm clothes. Our eyes locked, our fists clenched, and then I saw her foot move one inch forward.

Boxes and girls went flying! I landed upside down in the first bin, an old withered moon boot working its way up my left nostril. Next thing Jen was on my back ripping a blue hoodie out of my hands. After a well-placed elbow and a monster squat, I wobbled to my feet, somewhat able to half fling Jen into the second bin. In one of my signature displays of immaturity, I then grabbed the sweatshirt out of her hands and yelled, "Mine!" This went back and forth for several minutes until we were both flung apart, out across the floor, landing in the mess we had made of the room. I jerked my head around as I scrambled to my feet, blood hot in my ears (this was fun!), and only then noticed the wide eyes and open mouths of the rest of the bystanders. A giggle escaped one of them. The laughter was inevitable, signaling the end of the game, which was fine because it was too damn exhausting to keep up. Helping Jen to her feet, both of our faces flushed and our bodies banged up from the ruckus, I conceded to giving her some of the better items. After all, I had ten years on her and didn't mind settling for the "less cool" of the clothes.

This behemoth mound of crap puzzled me until I gazed along a bulging side of one of the boxes and landed on the words: "Take Me." Photo by Amanda Chavira. Courtesy of Laura Katers.

In the end, my share was a pair of tight, stonewashed jeans, blue sweatpants, a Penn State sweatshirt, and a white ski coat with a large, fake fur collar. All items felt worn and well lived. The obnoxious fur coat went everywhere with me for the next month, including to the bedroom. After that, I moved north, to the tropics of Queensland, and to the brim of another bin. There I traded the coat for a tank top, an umbrella, and a green canvas belt I used to hold up a pair of huge hiking shorts that once belonged to a man from Madrid.

Packing for the three-month trip had equated to one of those beautifully uncomfortable moments: sifting through material possessions—

the greatest proof of one's existence—in order to get to the bare essentials. At home, in Colorado, I'd spent an entire weekend rifling through the mounds of crap congealed to the insides of my closet and dresser drawers, and had made double sure to check the boxes in the garage. What would I take, if I couldn't take it all?

The first time I went backpacking, six years earlier, I'd packed enough gear for a small family. I was satisfied with myself until I walked that first awkward and painful mile. It was only then that I discovered the true weight of my most precious belongings. Backpacking was my first lesson in personal freedom. It was the first time I looked at material goods based not on what I wanted but on what I *needed*. They were, in fact, not the same thing. Soon after this realization came the next—that my long established "gotta-have-everything" and "gotta-have-the-best" mentality just wasn't healthy.

Case in point: my last and only pair of Smith sunglasses. I'd coughed up one hundred dollars for the frames and three sets of lenses. One week after the Smiths were on my face, I was in California on a pontoon boat, clenching a large Super Soaker in my cold, white fists. My friends and I were "at war" with another boat. As I was leaning toward the water for a refill, I felt something slide off my face. Only when I saw the Smiths dipping below the murky waters below did I realize what had happened.

I launched myself overboard.

With the pontoon jetting along at a good clip, I was quickly left behind in frigid waters—with no life preserver. To make matters worse, I landed on my face, swallowing enough lake water to fill a lung. A friend dove in, thinking my antic was accidental—which I did maintain afterward, at least until someone asked me where my sunglasses were. Then word was out that Laura had nearly killed herself for a piece of expensive plastic. Near death aside, I couldn't help but brood the rest of the day. "Never again!"

On the way home from that same trip, a package of mine disappeared in transit from LAX to DIA. More brooding. Then I finally accepted that we never actually own anything. I was borrowing those sunglasses, just like I am borrowing everything else I think I own. So why not focus on acquiring used items? This practice would almost immediately save me money, headaches, self-inflicted injuries, and also space in the end. When I gain a new item, I am giving it away to one place, inevitably. The landfill. Or the bottom of a lake in California.

I had brought only the essentials with me to Australia, nothing more. Prolonged sickness, or even imminent death, would've been unlikely had I not stumbled upon the bins, but they did save me, or rather, they salvaged an idea that I, and my people, seemed to have forgotten long ago. The idea of a culture that believes in simplicity—taking, yes taking, but also giving back. The idea of a culture that understands that once we use something up, or throw something away, it's gone.

And maybe, in small ways, I'd been learning this all along. Years ago I told my folks to never buy me knickknacks again, only things that I can wear into the woods, read, or eat. My favorite gift would still be getting something made from something else: poems, a coffee table made out of fallen lumber, a bookshelf made from scrapped and snapped skis, a clock made of bike sprockets and chains, photos of places I can only imagine seeing for myself.

After my teaching commitment in Australia was up, I had a month left to explore. I hit the hostel circuit straightaway and was further astounded to find all sorts of bins, in all shapes and sizes. Some empty, some exploding. The best find was the food bin located at a rambunctious hostel along the Gold Coast. Most hostels, I quickly found, had a special shelf or place in the fridge for "throwaway" food. If your time was up and you'd rather not carry a sack of groceries on the plane or bus or while hitching, you simply tossed it on this shelf. Then it was up for grabs. I was one of five or so travelers who would wake daily at seven o'clock to check for goods. There was never much, but it always seemed enough. Half boxes of stale cereal, wine, dehydrated milk, rice, cooking oil, peanut butter, raisins, sugar, tea, and coffee. I was thrilled—amazed actually—that I was able to survive off the bins, off items that would've otherwise turned to waste.

I immediately envisioned various community bins adorning corners in every downtown back home. Bins full of food; full of down coats maybe. Instead of buying a new coat for the handful of ridiculously frigid Front Range days, why not simply borrow one and then toss it back in the heap for someone else to use? It was a far-fetched idea, throwing out such overused and somewhat obsessive ideals as hygiene and fashion, but functionally, and financially, it did make sense.

Was I embarrassed going through someone else's leftovers? Well, the thought certainly had crossed my mind. Did I feel like a bum? A scavenger? I thought about that too, but I also thought about something else. I was saving money. If I spent less money, then I didn't need as much, and if I didn't need as much, I could travel that much longer. Which I did.

Growing up, I was always told that I was too sensitive. *Everything* had feelings in my strange little world, even the living room carpet; even clothes that didn't fit anymore. If the childhood carpet had feelings, and clothes and books and boxes had feelings (and I still feel this way, but I think I've gotten used to ignoring their cries), one can imagine the drama that ensued while I sat with my mostly borrowed belongings—spread out like treasure across my dorm room floor—that last night in the Southern Hemisphere. Unfortunately for me, my Italian friend, Alice, was trying to rid herself of her borrowed treasures as well—many of which I had been eye-balling for weeks.

"You want my ballet?" she asked, innocently enough, holding up a tight, black, but very nice and somewhat silky, long-sleeved shirt with "ballet" splattered across the front in shiny sequined lettering. Such a shirt would normally make me want to hurl, but it was one of our "going out" shirts—one that we traded back and forth, worn when we wanted to "look pretty." There were memories sealed into that cotton thread! Realistically, I probably wouldn't wear it, but . . . maybe . . . I could keep it . . . in a box . . . for. . . .

"No," I said, with force. "Put it in the bin."

And so it went for two beer-filled hours. I'd used the hell out of those things, to the point where they held more sentimental value than anything I'd brought from home. I took more items from Alice's pile, and then put them back. Keeping the memories is what I craved, but then the thought of finding those clothes in my garage, probably serving as mouse nests, made me cringe. I wanted them, more than anything, to be of use to someone else.

When I finally returned to America, my perception had been altered permanently, as any extended trip will usually do. I found myself swearing often, feeling anxious and disgusted upon reacquainting myself with the landscape of my native country—and then with my savagely stuffed storage unit. I have never owned much, but suddenly everything I did have seemed like too much. The shadows of goods in that cold, steel locker mocked me: "Where you gonna put me, silly girl? Thought you could lose us, didn't you!"

Then I began to protest outwardly, uttering bits of disbelief at the madness of humans consuming anything not bolted to the ground (and sometimes even bolts could not stop them) just for the sake of satisfying the unappeasable hunger to own more things than we can ever find room for. Where will all of these things go when we are gone anyway? Who will own them? What kind of space will they take up? Most of us already know.

The native people of Australia, and one of the oldest living cultures in the world, could withstand some of the harshest environments known to humankind—those of the dead, red center of the outback. The Aboriginal people lived in communion with the land, essentially basing their survival on one common practice that our current civilization seems to struggle with. If they picked all the seeds and fruits from a certain area, the seeds and fruits were gone. There would be nothing left for the hungry and thirsty to come after, and, more importantly, there would be nothing left for them the next time they needed it. Just enough was taken to sustain the individuals present, no more. Fruits and plants were left to grow, to continue to cultivate and thrive in an area. Traditionally, the Aboriginals knew the land so well, and knew enough to not use an area until it was arable, that they were able to survive the most ruthless of elements and cross impossible distances with extraordinarily meager rations. It was the only way they knew to keep the balance between the living, the dying, and the future of both. There are tribes in remote parts of Australia that still follow these long-established practices, but their land—and their knowledge of it—is quickly disappearing.

These days, I sometimes celebrate the same shirt every day, shower infrequently, and have dreams of growing a beard like Jeremiah Johnson and living off of the land, taking only what I need and leaving the rest to propagate, grow, and nourish other lives and seasons. I am delighted to discover how little I can actually get by on, avoiding excess as best I can, having succumbed to living on pretty meager rations—realizing full well that *my* meager may not be the same as another's. But I feel full, more full, the fullest maybe ever.

Second Thoughts

ELLEN SANTASIERO

Ellen Santasiero grew up in New York and Indiana. In 1989, she moved west, where she learned that the word "butte" was not pronounced "butt." Her essays typically revolve around her lifelong experience with depression; this is the first piece she's written about her attempts to live more sustainably. Her essays and author interviews have appeared in *The Sun, Northwest Review, Marlboro Review*, and *High Desert Journal*. She was the 2006–07 Scholar in Residence at Central Oregon Community College in Bend and is on the editorial board of *High Desert Journal*.

When my husband and I built our house, we both wanted to use recycled materials and insulate the place as much as we could. I hadn't always understood why it was important to recycle or conserve heat, but living with John had taught me a whole new way to live, one that was less consumptive in every way. Now, we agree about composting kitchen scraps, eating organic, and buying second-hand. And though it took me longer to get ready for it, we were both excited to get rid of our car and become bicycle commuters.

But when John started bringing home clothing he had found in the bike lane—and actually wearing them—I balked. He could have gotten the same items at a secondhand store, and I wouldn't have said a word. Who knows, the clothes might have actually been *on their way* to the secondhand store when they accidentally fell out of the back of someone's pickup! But for some reason, I just didn't like it. Like a child, I basically regarded the clothes as *icky*. They had been on the ground, like litter. Worse, they had been in the *gutter*. I remember my parents and grandparents using that word: the gutter was dirty, they said, and so were the things found in it.

Also, I associated the clothes—a pair of men's khakis and a month later, a pair of men's jeans—with furtive and gamey sex. Not my own, though. After all, decades earlier, a boyfriend and I had had sex on a dune in Cape Cod, and afterwards he cleaned himself up with his boxers and then buried them in the sand. When my husband came into the kitchen and unfurled the pants from his bike bag and announced where he had found them, my mind unearthed that memory of the beach. Who knew the history of the khakis John was now holding up to his waist?

Maybe my resistance stemmed from another memory, one more dangerous than icky. When I was very young, four or five, I found a pen in the gutter out in front of our suburban house on Long Island. I brought it inside to show my grandmother, who began fiddling with it. Into my face squirted mace, burning, so they say, my eyes and skin. If the pants John found were possibly unclean or held hidden dangers, why would I want to touch them? John, however, was thrilled. He washed them up, tried them on. The khakis, and then the jeans, fit him just right. Two perfectly good pairs of pants for nothing!

When I ride my bike, I find things in the bike lane, too. Mostly building materials. Every nail, screw, washer, and unidentifiable piece of metal you could want is scattered there. I found a brand new utility knife one day and a tube of caulking another. Occasionally two-by-fours lie in wait. In a year's time, I see single gloves, hats, towels, clothing, and dead animals, but I don't stop for any of those things. John will pick up most everything, but he knows not to stop for the women's clothing or the dead animals. He once tried to keep a foam pillow with neck support, but I put that straight in the trash.

The bike lane is a place that drivers of cars and trucks don't even think about. To them, it doesn't really exist. Even when drivers use it, it's not the bike lane. It's the breakdown lane. Or the passing lane. The more we ride though, the more we realize the bike lane is not just a place for breaking down or passing or even cycling. It's a catchall, a holding place, an eddy that swirls with what is carelessly lost from the mainstream of an affluent society.

If you are part of the percentage of Americans that considers themselves to be environmentalists, you may have heard that the cotton industry in the United States is a dirty business all around. It's been accused of being a monocrop fed heavy helpings of synthetic pesticides and fertilizers. Critics say cotton here is typically farmed in soil stripped of nutrients that just serves to hold plants in place. Poison sprayed from overhead, some observers say, contaminates living things—including people—in adjacent fields. We have some idea about how surface water and groundwater are vulnerable to runoff and leaching, especially after hearing news reports in 2006 about E. coli–contaminated spinach in California. Where runoff does not drain to the sea, it creates large ponds that can potentially attract and harm migrating birds. We're alarmed, some of us, when we hear about pesticide-laden cottonseed oil ending up in our food and feed for livestock or about how toxic the dyeing process is.

Advocates of the nonorganic cotton industry claim it's not as bad as all that. They suspect that retailers such as organic cotton proponents Patagonia, Nike, and Walmart may be pushing organics just to cast a green light on their corporate faces. And that the demand for organic cotton is a trend, that consumers will want something else next year.

I don't know if any of the claims—for or against organic or nonorganic—are true. I don't do market research. I've never seen a cotton field; I've never met a cotton grower. But I do have my intuition. Eighty percent of the cotton grown in the United States stems from genetically modified organism (GMO) seed. Though people on both sides of the fence may disagree with me, I don't think we know much about the long-term effects of GMOs. But I don't want to risk it. My intuition about health compels me to reach for organic products instead of the nonorganic, the non-GMO goods instead of the GMOs.

As consumers and citizens who oppose the growing of non-organic cotton, we can do the obvious: we can inform ourselves about organic cotton (we can find out, for example, if it's true that it takes more land to grow organic cotton, as nonorganic cotton industry officials claim); we can buy only organic cotton; we can write our congresspeople; or we can reduce our demand for such dirty fabric by shopping—or gleaning—secondhand.

In order to make an impact on the cotton industry, second-hand shopping would have to happen on a large scale (the avail-ability of secondhand clothing, of course, relies on the availability of firsthand clothing, but that's another story). But it's not happening on a large scale. Why don't more people acquire secondhand clothing? Years back, I found a terrific black dress at a consignment shop, and I wore it to the graduation party for my master's program. A woman classmate complimented me on the dress, and when I told her I'd gotten it for twenty dollars at a secondhand store, she scolded, "Don't tell anyone that!" My mother, who shops second-hand, told me she never lets on to her best friend where she buys her clothes because she imagines her friend would be appalled. Those are just anecdotes, but they point to the shame many people feel buying or wearing anything less than brand-new. Wearing a hand-me-down, even if we selected it and purchased it ourselves, can feel regressive. Certainly, there is pleasure in finding a won-derful item secondhand, but it may remind some of us of being a child, powerless and denied the free agency of choosing all of our own stuff. New things tell the world that we are prosperous, and therefore, powerful. At the most fundamental level, though, surrounding ourselves with new things is a hedge against that final loss of power. Running our hands over the bright threads of a brand-new cotton sweater, it can be said, is like stroking an amulet we believe will bring us luck and a long, if not quite eternal, life.

I am a forty-five-year-old woman, but when I ride my bike, young people notice me. They smile or immediately start talking to me, either about the bike or the ride or the weather. They perceive me differently than when I show up in a car. An adult who rides a bike in all weather is a different kind of adult, someone they might want to talk to.

Those who ride bikes, like those who wear someone else's discarded clothing, are assumed to be children, or people who have no money, which amounts to the same thing. One time my husband and I pedaled by a road crew on our way to work, and one of the workers told us to get off the road, because, he claimed, we probably didn't pay taxes. But being perceived as a second-class citizen also erases you in some ways, and if you are shy like me, this is a welcome state of being. You can move in and around the world without being noticed too much. You are not a threat. The message is subliminal, and it goes something like this: if she gets mad at us, what is she going to do, ram us with her bike?

Homeless people are regarded this way, too: as powerless, certainly, and ineffective, at least by our standards (though they have a powerful effect on those who would see them). I meet homeless people in the bike lane, and just as I was glad to be suddenly in relationship with young people as I wheeled down the bike lane, at first I was glad to encounter homeless people there. Glad because in the past I never gave anything to beggars, and I felt guilty about that. It was easier to give once I was out from behind the glass, plastic, and steel of an automobile, balancing my bike right next to a person sitting on the curb. Now I feel more—

Homeless people are regarded this way, too: as powerless, certainly, and ineffec-tive, at least by our standards (though they have a powerful effect on those who would see them).

though certainly not completely—like a fellow traveler, and it's easier for me to talk to people, pet their dogs, and give them something.

But even though I now share a piece of the street with homeless people, I still feel dread when I see them up ahead on the corner and the stoplight is red. There are two ways to ride my bike to the grocery store. On the sweep of asphalt that leads me behind the store, I know that I will pass a homeless man, the blond one with the pitted skin who calls me "girl." I go the other way because I hate the helpless feeling I have when I see him. When I was a young woman, I organized the twentieth anniversary celebration of Earth Day in my town. I helped educate a lot of people (myself included) about environmental issues, but after two years, I left that work because I realized that environmental problems couldn't be solved until economic problems were solved. And since I left environmental work, I haven't done anything to create economic justice besides giving a few homeless people some of what I have. I'm not sure that's good enough.

I dread encountering the homeless for another reason, too: One day I gave a handful of dollars to a woman, my age, on the street. She grabbed not just the bills but my hand, and held it and squeezed it in gratitude for a few long moments. I am ashamed to admit that I kept that hand away from my face until I could get to a sink and wash it. When people aren't able to wash, as many homeless people can't, I always assume they have some kind of sickness. What if that woman had a disease, I remember thinking, as she released my hand, and what if she's given it to me? It was then I realized that the reason I won't wear found clothing is that I'm always afraid that it once belonged to a homeless person. This fear is born of a faulty logic—itself born of a set of appalling assumptions gone unexamined until now—but it's my logic nevertheless: if I wear clothing worn by a homeless person, I might get lice or crabs or some other communicable condition. I will buy and wear second-hand clothes, though, because I believe in the trusty filter of the secondhand store, where clothes likely come from homes and are vetted and laundered by others. Finally, I don't want to wear clothes that may have belonged to a homeless person because I am afraid they are infused with the bad luck of the wearer. It's hard for me to ride my bicycle past homeless people, let alone pull their mantles of despair around my shoulders.

My husband does fine, though. No diseases have claimed him since he started wearing found clothes. He and I both know there is always the chance that I will one day think differently about found clothing. After all, my husband points out, I've come a long way from the suburban girl I was, who used to only buy new clothes. He thinks it's just short of a miracle that I'm in the bike lane at all.

"Look," my husband said recently, coming through the door with a garment folded up in his hand. "I found something for you."

He pulled out a burgundy-colored apron, clearly part of someone's uniform at a fast-food restaurant. It had a silver buckle to adjust the neck strap and appeared to be a woman's size and was in good shape. I smiled. We both laughed. He knows I won't wear it, at least not yet. And not just because I already have an apron. I won't put it in the trash, though. I will instead put it in the laundry, and then fold it in a drawer as a backup, just in case I change my mind.

Every Popsicle Stick Counts

KATHY LYNN HARRIS

Kathy Lynn Harris grew up amidst the hot, mesquite-covered flatlands of South Texas, surrounded by a family of hardworking, larger-than-life characters who often fuel her fiction, poetry, and nonfiction writing today. "Every Popsicle Stick Counts" pays tribute to her grandmother, one of those legendary women you simply don't cross if you know what's good for you. Kathy now makes her home high in the Colorado mountains along the Continental Divide—where she puts her (and her grandmother's) respect for the land to use through conservation and letters to the editor.

My grandmother on my father's side would have rather slept with the Devil than join forces with any kind of hippie-based, peace-love-back-to-earth movement.

Let's just say Granny was quite the tough Texas ranchwoman. A five-foot-tall force to be reckoned with. A woman who could stare down a nine-hundred-pound Brahma bull in a pen the size of her kitchen in the morning, then fix collard greens and cornbread, still wearing her rubber farm boots, in the afternoon.

Let's just say Granny was quite the tough Texas ranchwoman. A five-foot-tall force to be reckoned with. A woman who could stare down a nine-hundred-pound Brahma bull in a pen the size of her kitchen.

She was also a woman who, unlike me, didn't spend a great deal of time worrying about the future of our country's landfills, reading the current research on greenhouse gases, or considering whether a Sonic Drive-In take-out cup was in any way biodegradable. I can guarantee she didn't care one iota about karma, good or bad. And if she were alive today, I think she'd get a pretty good chuckle out of me and my sometimes loudly verbalized convictions about saving the environment—and would no doubt shake her head at how much time and effort I put into recycling newspapers and Dr. Pepper bottles.

Yet my grandmother remains the one person who taught me the most about conservation and reuse.

Granted, she didn't use those terms or bother to label her daily actions. And she sure as hell would never admit to sharing parallel values with anyone who relishes the use of hemp. She just knew reusing was the smart thing to do.

One of my first lessons in reuse from Granny involved a rather hot summer afternoon—and a wooden Popsicle stick still wet with purple stains. I remember aiming that stick at the trash can, intent on tossing it away quickly before those evil South Texas fire ants covered it, and my hand, in their fiery red stings. That's when my grandmother promptly yanked the stick from my hand with her own calloused one, and gave me a look that would've made a preacher feel guilty.

"What?" I asked, hand on hip and with a bit more sass than I could usually get away with around my grandmother. I was feeling brave.

She didn't answer me, just faced me with a raised eyebrow and a tightly drawn mouth. I knew that face—and that face was never a particularly good sign. She proceeded to guide me not-so-gently by the elbow to the kitchen sink, where she stood behind my shoulder, forcing me to wash that one stick with green Palmolive soap until every trace of stickiness was gone. Then she took it from me, dried it with a kitchen towel, and dropped it into a brown paper grocery sack that held at least fifty other sticks just like mine.

Two months later, my whole family had Popsicle-stick picture frames, and Granny had me working alongside her in the garden, labeling new fall plants with Popsicle-stick garden stakes. I'm fairly sure that's where I learned how to spell "cauliflower," which was written sideways on a stick, along with the planting date.

In my grandmother's eyes, it was always quite simple. You didn't throw anything—*anything*—away. Because there was always another use for it. And if a new use wasn't apparent right then, you'd keep the item just in case. Besides, there wasn't money to pay for a constant supply of new things, and you never knew when you might need what you just tossed away.

For many years of my young life, Granny still wore those old flour-sack cotton dresses, made from the floral fabric sacks of flour of the 1930s and 1940s. Those dresses were as tough as my grandmother, lasting decades without deteriorating. She didn't care that wearing such a thing spoke of Depression poverty or that it might say a great deal more about her sense of style or lack thereof. (She wouldn't hesitate, however, to dress it all up with a pair of strappy white sandals, if there were a community party to attend.)

Today, as I look around my little log cabin located here in the mountains of Colorado, so far from my family's land and my heritage in South Texas, I have to shake my head. The floor is covered with piles of things I've collected with grand hopes of recycling— items I'll eventually take down to Denver on a once-a-month recycling drop. The number of aluminum and steel cans alone makes me cringe. Just two weeks' worth takes up far too much space and tells me just how often we Americans use containers like these only once and then chuck them without another thought.

I doubt my grandmother ever even heard of a recycling center in her rural area. But she certainly had her own recycling program: she made sure just about everything she acquired had a second, third, or forever use. (The most impressive of which, by the way, was to cut aluminum beer cans into pieces and stitch them together with crochet yarn to make funny little hats. I have pictures to prove this.)

I remember Granny would buy those generic-brand two-liter bottles of soda to have on hand for us kids. Inevitably, we'd find those empty plastic bottles all over her house and yard, used in a multitude of creative manners—cut in half and used to protect young plants in her garden, made into a weird kind of shower caddy for the bathroom, or sitting beside her favorite chair in the living room, keeping her crochet yarn from tangling as she worked on her next project.

Where there wasn't plastic being reused, there was glass. Used bottles and jars of all kinds lined the garage utility shelves—themselves old 2 x 4 slats of wood from some torn-down shed. The jars were stacked neatly and arranged by size, to later be used as flower vases and incubators for cuttings of ivy and other plants. Or as containers to hold nails. And screws. And bolts. She also used jars like these over and over again for canning vegetables and fruit every year, for making her homemade jellies and jams. I plucked many a sweet pickle, made from her garden cucumbers, out of an old spaghetti sauce jar.

And those little round margarine containers? They soon became "I Can't Believe It's Not Tupperware" in her refrigerator, their contents labeled over and over again in black marker.

She also didn't believe in throwing away old and broken-down appliances. She'd fix them with secondhand parts. Or she'd find another use. At one point, she placed a defunct clothes dryer in the hay barn as some sort of storage unit.

Would she discard cardboard boxes? Please. I remember her reshaping a box that once held store-bought cookies into a bunk bed for my Barbie dolls. If a larger box crossed her path, she'd tear it down and add it to a pile she kept under old blankets in the garage to keep her outdoor cats warm and comfy at night.

When clothes didn't fit anymore or were so worn they had holes in them, she'd remove the buttons or snaps and cut the fabric into cleaning rags and dish towels. I still do this myself all the time, especially with my husband's ratty old T-shirts. When it comes time to dust the house, he'll pull out a rag and quickly recognize bits and pieces of his 311 concert shirt from 1999. He rarely finds this amusing.

Granny also used old clothes as fabric patches for quilts and handmade oddities. (This is where Granny and I differ the most. I couldn't patch together a quilt if my life depended on it.)

We often ate lunch with Granny after working cattle, and it was usually a quick sandwich on white bread. Even then we all understood to save those plastic bread bags and the plastic-covered wire bread ties. To this day, I'm not sure how she used those wire bread ties, but there must have been hundreds tucked around the house.

Although my grandmother was a hardy, year-round gardener, I doubt she ever heard of a compost pile. She did, however, make sure that after each meal, we tossed our leftovers into the ever-present slop bucket. Depending on the contents, she'd either toss the leftovers into her garden, or toss it over the fence for the cats or the horse or the wild animals.

Probably unknowingly, Granny also inspired her neighbors to reuse. Many would drop off items to her—old automobile or tractor parts, segments of hay strings, unused reams of fabric, potential canning jars—that they thought she could find some use for. And she usually did. She acquired numerous plastic buckets that she then placed around her backyard to catch scarce rainwater, which was then used to water her indoor plants.

My grandmother has been gone for several years now. But her beliefs in gleaning all we can from all we encounter are alive and well, if only in my own attempts to salvage and recycle even the smallest of items. I wash and reuse pieces of foil and those pint-sized plastic food storage bags. I have far more than my share of margarine, yogurt, and sour cream containers stacked in my kitchen cabinets. I drive my husband crazy storing junk-mail paper that I use as notepads. Spaghetti sauce, peanut butter, and pickle jars are washed of their labels and ready for reuse. I shop the thrift stores and yard sales when I can. I look for used items online. I can't stand to throw vegetable scraps or corn husks or apple peels into a plastic garbage bag, so I pitch them out into the meadow behind our house for the deer, elk, and rabbits to eat, if they're so inclined. I even save those little wire bread ties, though I still don't know why and have yet to actually reuse one.

In fact, in recent years, the art of reusing has even become a slight obsession with me—a personal challenge of some sort. Before tossing anything, I try to take a moment to think about how it could be used again. I don't always succeed, but I guess a part of me hopes that my efforts will make my grandmother just a bit proud of me and my damn-near-hippie lifestyle. And perhaps, along the way, I'm making a tiny difference in preserving the environment for my infant son to enjoy as he grows up and has children of his own one day—*my* grandchildren.

I'm well aware, of course, that my grandmother didn't take on her philosophy of frugality and reuse because of any highfalutin idea of saving the earth for future generations. She learned that way of life from her parents and grandparents, from years of finding it difficult to put money in the bank, and from the only lifestyle she ever knew—farming and ranching.

Being inventive with everything that crossed her path meant she survived another month, or another year, of working a drought-ridden, unforgiving land in an unpredictable economy. A strong sense of necessity drove many of her actions and decisions. In contrast, I have a quite comfortable and predictable life.

But I also believe that somewhere beneath my grandmother's no-nonsense side, there was a soft and unspoken, perhaps even whimsical, respect that guided her choices—a respect not only for the land and its role in her daily life but also for the people who provided and packaged the items she couldn't grow or make herself. Because she made so much by hand, and labored long hours to manage and generate livestock and produce, she understood that every item, every person, every blade of grass, every drop of rain, had value. And it was only right to honor that.

In short, you don't throw away a perfectly good Popsicle stick just because the icy grape treat is gone. That wood came from somewhere important. And in her eyes, pitching it out as mere garbage was like sticking your purple tongue out at the universe. (Okay, so maybe Granny wouldn't have used the term, "universe," but you get the idea.)

Of Rags and Bags

LIBBY JAMES

Because of a dad with itchy pants, Libby James spent her childhood between England, Washington, D.C., New York, Seattle, and Philadelphia, but for the last forty years, Colorado has been her anchor. She has a master's degree in western American literature from Colorado State University and has written features for newspapers and magazines. She likes to run, bike, write, and play with tea bags and with her twelve grandchildren.

Maybe it's because I grew up in the suburbs of London before and after World War II when scarcity was a fact of life. Or maybe it's in my DNA, inherited from an English grandmother who was widowed young and raised four children on practically nothing. "I'm a widow with four children," she would explain to salesclerks, always with the expectation of a lower price for her purchase.

Whatever the reason, I've had a lifelong affinity for frugality and the quirky habits that go along with squeezing every possible bit of value out of what I own. I cut toothpaste tubes in half and scoop out the remains, save chicken bones to make soup, and have to monitor my ever-growing plastic container collection carefully.

My love affair with compost is related to my penchant for making things do double duty. I get a kick out of depositing food scraps in a corner of my yard and watching them—with the help of worms, weather, and a little water—turn into a nutritious, aerating addition to my garden. That which once had no value, in time, becomes something of value.

Several years ago I bought my son Jeff a birthday card that was so funny that I didn't sign it. Instead I wrote him a note on a separate piece of paper suggesting that because this was such a great card, I wasn't going to mess it up by signing it. He could send it to someone else. In a few days, it came back to me with "consider it used" scribbled across it. I saved it and sent it to him for his birthday the next winter. The next summer, he sent it back to me—and on it went for ten years.

Some of my clothes are very old—including a red nylon windbreaker that has been part of my wardrobe for fifty-seven years, given to me by my parents when I was thirteen. In fact, perhaps it is this jacket that I have used the most, and loved the most. A yellowed shoelace replaces the original drawstring for the hood. Seams gap open here and there, causing little wisps of fraying red fabric to dangle from a sleeve and a shoulder. On the pocket flap, I prize the small holes where ski tow tickets were once stapled.

Soon nylon windbreakers were eclipsed by down, Gore-Tex, polypropylene, and polar fleece. Where a heavy sweater under a windbreaker was once sufficient, now it seems you need a "system" consisting of several layers of just the right kind of wicking, waffled, wind-resistant fabric. But I have sweated up Pikes Peak and down the Grand Canyon on my two feet and ridden from Iowa to Maine on two skinny wheels. Like an old friend, my jacket stuck with me.

I never gave a thought to getting rid of Old Red until I was presented with a stylish red fleece pullover at a marathon in Steamboat Springs, Colorado, in 2000. Here was some worthy competition for my oldest piece of clothing that by now had arrived at the half-century mark. But I couldn't do it. I couldn't bring myself to relegate my frayed red rag to the Dumpster, or even to the Goodwill

The hardest things to get rid of, next to the things you think you might need one day, are things that have been given to you by a good friend, things that conjure up fond memories.

pile. We have too many memories together. So I keep my grand old rag, a symbol of good times and, some would say, irrational frugality.

I try not to let my "hang onto it" propensities get the best of me. I like to think of myself as a minimalist—as someone who keeps only what is needed and useful. I believe collecting stuff for its own sake is a disease with dire consequences—frustration, outrageous consumption of valuable time, inefficiency, and often full-blown depression. I have friends who have been trying to pare down their possessions ever since I've known them, all the while shopping away (which compounds their dilemma).

I love these friends, and I think I understand them. The hardest things to get rid of, next to the things you think you might need one day, are things that have been given to you by a good friend, things that conjure up fond memories, trigger a story, or recall a wedding, vacation, or accomplishment. How can you throw away the chipped pottery bowl a son made in kindergarten or the blurry black and white photos your uncle took in Singapore?

Every toss requires a painful decision, one we may never be ready to make. Despite my determination to give new life to twisty ties, rubber bands, old shoelaces, and yogurt containers, two things help me to toss when it's time: I moved a lot when I was a kid, and I live in a very small house. My need for frugality and my need for simplicity keep the balance.

I drink lots of tea. I grew up with a mom who believed that a cup of tea could cure anything—sore throats, stomach aches, hypothermia, even insomnia. Every day two or three bags ended up in my compost pile—but no longer, because I've found a way to give them value. Now I make tea bag art.

I started making tea bag art when I fell in love with a design on a used tea bag glued to a notecard I received. The greeting read, "Once filled with tea . . . Now filled with love." One day in a fit of faux creativity, I slashed open a Celestial Seasonings tea bag I'd soaked to extinction and shook out the soggy contents. A slightly stained square of porous fabric pinched together at the edges by a tiny serrated border remained, dangling from my fingers.

I averaged a C in art every year I was in school until I didn't have to take art any more. I possess some limited skills with a pen, such as making very small dots and drawing lines. But the tea bags are different. What I do with tea bags, glitter, and paint is not art, but it is *something*—craft, dogged perseverance, procrastination from more onerous tasks. I don't know. What I know is that I can spend hours designing and creating artsy little squares and rectangles that look surprisingly pleasant mounted on a notecard and surrounded by a simple gold or black inked frame. Sometimes I add words like, "Old Bags are Best," "Old tea bags never die. They just get dressed up," or "Happy Bag Day."

I began to experiment with different kinds of bags. Celestial Seasonings seemed the best choice, as they are unencumbered by staples and strings and are a convenient, square shape. But I discovered that stringed and stapled bags work just as well. Some bags are delivered to me by friends after a week or so in a plastic bag, vaguely smelly and beginning to mold. The stains on these aged bags inspire abstract designs. The first time I saw pink bags, stained by hibiscus or Red Zinger tea, I was ready to reject them. But I found that the deep pink provides a dramatic background for black and silver markings. In this way, rejuvenating tea bags has become my passion—one that satisfies my reuse gene and feeds an ever-lurking entrepreneurial bent as well.

I've sold enough "oldbags" that I now have a few coins to keep me supplied with blank notes, glitter, markers, and glue. Meanwhile, I'm drinking more tea than I ever have in my life, and there are no bags, only tons of tea leaves flying out my back door into the compost pile.

Using up and reusing defines me, I guess. I think it satisfies something deep inside me to see how long an item can remain useful and to figure out new ways to use things that would otherwise meet their end in the trash heap.

It's easy to exchange money (if you have enough) for new clothes or for printed notecards. But I think I'll go on using and reusing, hanging on to my old clothes, and saving tea bags to make note-cards. And maybe, in some small way, the world will be a better place.

Less

SHANE E. BONDI

Shane E. Bondi is a writer of fiction and nonfiction, a painter of still lifes, and an illustrated journalist (that is, the journals are illustrated, not the journalist). She's pedaled her bicycle across this country for several years, during which time she's contemplated—in addition to many discarded recyclables—many discarded or plain unlucky armadillos, snakes, prairie dogs, and other fodder for the grilles of motorists. This essay takes her on a new journey of contemplation: to her first landfill and experiment into the hierarchy of reduce, reuse, recycle. This is her first published essay.

Out here, at Colorado's Larimer County Landfill Garbage Garage, Hilda is in charge. She looks like anyone's grandma, but she's yelling at this group of kids like she's a drill sergeant. "You're in sixth grade! What does recycling *mean?*"

The group of kids, at first merely crowded together, now seem to huddle closer. There is silence for at least thirty seconds.

"*What does recycling mean?*"

One kid ventures, finally, "To use again?"

"No!" Hilda bellows, "That's *RE-USE!* Think! If we recycle it, what do we *do* with it? *Think!*"

Another long silence, and I'm glad I'm not part of this group, hidden as I am with my notebook behind the "Mountain of Trash"— an indoor shed covered with things like stringless guitars, a bottle of Coppola Chardonnay (Vintage 2001), a scale that looks like it got tossed when it told its owner some 260 pounds of bad news, a golf bag, Christmas ornaments, unpaired shoes, computer parts, stuffed animals, and coat hangers. I'm frightened for the kids as well as for myself.

The answer is to make something new out of something old, she finally has to tell the group, and I'm sure the shame on their faces is mirrored on my own. It just sounds so darn easy.

It probably wasn't the best day for me to be here; there have been 140 school kids shuttled in groups of about twenty through this Garbage Garage, receiving instructions from Hilda to spend fifteen minutes and come back having learned at least one thing. They roam around, pushing buttons, marveling at the "Mountain of Trash," and reading the displays and information on the walls. I've been wandering around myself for over an hour. Though the room isn't large, there's a lot to look at. One group reconvenes, and Hilda picks a kid—I'm overhearing from where I'm taking notes off a wall placard about how to make everything from toothpaste to toilet bowl cleaner with baking soda—and asks him what he learned. The kid says nothing. She demands that he must have learned *something.* I hear a small, frightened voice piping out something obviously ineffectual.

"You're in sixth grade! Surely you can *read?* You *can* read, can't you?" She berates him to such an extent I'm wondering if the kid will wet his pants. I think I would. She tells him he's got one minute to walk around again and learn something, and she's going to come back to him. The next victim puts her tidbit out there like it's a shield against a death ray. Something about Windex bottles—I was too anxious about the other boy to pay attention. He shows up again, and Hilda accosts him. He survives by telling Hilda in a wavering voice that glass is infinitely recyclable, but I imagine he might feel a little bit like some of those crushed soda cans on the wall.

Hilda is the real deal, as it turns out. She's wearing teal polyester pants, a drooping tan cardigan, a Larimer County Landfill T-shirt, huge glasses, and some of the ugliest brown sneakers I've ever seen. "Everything I'm wearing is secondhand," she tells me, gesturing down at herself, "except my underwear." She's a Depression-era kid, a Colorado kid, a farmer's kid, she says. Water has always been a precious resource to her. I ask her why she thinks Americans are worse than people in other countries, why we're so inclined toward overconsumption and waste. She says, emphatically, gesturing without looking at the kids milling around, "That's what they're taught from the day they were born! Their generation is the worst! They gotta have what they want when they want it!" She mentions some of the clothes they wear, and I immediately take mental inventory of what I'm wearing, embarrassed that all of my clothes were purchased firsthand. I'm thinking my beat-up backpack looks used enough to allow me at least a slightly more temperate level of hell. She lets out a whistle loud enough to make me wince and gathers the next group of victims—I mean kids—for interrogation—I mean questions.

There's no reason, I learn in the three hours I spend in the Garbage Garage—listening, reading, talking—to be soft on this issue.

I'm one of the worst. I live in a one-bedroom apartment, and I have four trash cans. Since moving to Colorado from Oregon, where recycling centers are found at every single grocery store and deposits are charged on cans and bottles, I had been throwing away my empties. Which I produced a lot of. It doesn't matter that I cringed a little each time I tossed a can in the garbage; I still did it.

But lately, I've been trying. My mountain of recyclable goods
has grown intimidating, not to mention incriminating, while garbage in the cans is slow to accumulate. I get angry at the mailman
now, for bringing me *so much* crap I have to find a way to deal
with it, instead of tossing it out. There's a number you can call to
stop a large portion of junk mail from ending up in your mailbox,
but they require you to punch in your Social Security number, so
I balk. I had a post office box in Oregon and received very little
junk mail, so I could check into getting one here. For the time
being, though, I still have reams of the stuff. My first idea, since
camping season had arrived, is to fill the envelopes from bulk mail
or bills with wadded paper and tie them up with twine, making
fire starters. I feel a little like a three-year-old, but it's something. I
move up to maybe the level of a fourth grader shortly after that,
however, by going online and finding out how to make paper. I
actually manage to get rid of an egg carton, some shredded paper,
and most of the week's mail, blending it up and making it into pathetic, flat little blobs of wet pulp. Of course, I had to buy a screen from
Home Depot, which was wrapped in plastic, as was the sponge,
and I unthinkingly put my three purchases, which I had quite
capably been carrying around the store, into a plastic bag for the
walk back to my car. I should have biked over, and I should have
used one of my knit shopping bags, or just, I don't know, carried the
stuff out? "Place your item in the bag," the self-checkout machine
said. I obeyed.

Probably the most horrifying thing I learn at the Garbage Garage—
and there are a lot of shocking numbers and facts—is what happens
to the e-waste of the United States. The Basel Action Network is a
group that acts to lessen the devastating impact of toxic dumping
by rich nations into poor nations. The world is our trash can, as it
turns out; the United States joins Russia, Malta, and Israel with
the shameful distinction of being the only notable countries that
refuse to ratify the treaties setting guidelines for environmentally

and ethically acceptable e-waste disposal. We send our toxic waste to places like China, India, and Pakistan, to areas without environmental protection. Even the EPA refuses to act on this global ethics crisis; we keep dumping our trash into the laps of unprotected and poverty-stricken human beings. A regular computer monitor contains three to eight pounds of lead; other harmful chemicals released in improper disposal of electronic products include bromine, chromium, cadmium, and mercury. In 1999 alone, twenty-four million computers became outdated; only three million were recycled.

It's depressing. But there are odder things to learn at the Garbage Garage, too. On a different level entirely, should a person need to dispose of a dead pet, or, say, a dead circus elephant, the fee is $5.60 per fifty pounds. Several years back, a circus was indeed in town; their elephant indeed died; its remains are indeed part of the Larimer County Landfill.

My day at the landfill is over. Hilda is getting ready to leave when the last of the kids shuffle out with their souvenir recycled-from-paper pencils. I get a chance to ask her what she likes best about her time at the Garbage Garage. "I love the kids!" she barks, and I dare not question her.

I am thrilled and dismayed by the information I find at the landfill. I'm the type of person who does things she's not supposed to do, and doesn't do things she should, waiting for something utterly concrete to drop on my head and show me the consequences of my actions, for better or worse. I couldn't visualize a final resting place for my garbage beyond the Dumpster in back of my apartment, because I'd never followed along behind the trucks after they collected it. I'd never trundled up the dirt hill behind the catchall fence, never realized the place looked like something out of a border-control documentary with its scuttling pieces of trash and pathetic clumps of weeds.

When I finally do drive to the landfill to watch the dump trucks dump and the personal vehicles with trailers unload onto the dirt mountain, the people with shovels looking disgusted, depressed, and guilty—unless I'm projecting—it smells, oddly enough, like the inside of the trash can when you take the bag of garbage out. Out to the Dumpster, out to the truck, out to the landfill.

This is exactly what I've been looking for: hard evidence. What dismays me is the damage I've done; that a significant part of that pile of garbage out here under the widening gyres of seagulls is directly my fault.

It's time to change—my foray into the trash heap and landfill has confirmed it. But beyond the obvious awareness that I *should* be recycling, reusing, and reducing, I realize that awareness needs to go deeper. I've been to Whole Foods with my little knit grocery bag, and I've bought my organic almonds and Nancy's Organic yogurt and strolled around in my sanctimonious haze, not knowing that the containers for this seemingly righteous food are not recyclable in Fort Collins.

In the same vein, industrial-sized fluorescent bulbs, which are so energy-efficient and environmentally friendly, come packaged in heavy plastic, also not recyclable at the landfill or recycling center in my town of Fort Collins. Both are set up for types 1 and 2 plastics; neither the yogurt container nor the bulb container qualifies.

Sometimes it's overwhelming, trying to be aware. I bought some pretzels from the vending machine on the Colorado State campus the other day. After eating them, I studied the three options for the package's disposal: a regular garbage can (more for the seagulls out at the landfill) and two recycling bins. My pretzel wrapper was shiny and crinkly. Plastic? Paper? What *was* it? There was a little number 6 on the bag, next to a tiny triangle that could have been a recycling symbol. It occurred to me, as I put the bag in my backpack to worry about later, that maybe some things are just garbage. And that I should think about that *before* I buy something.

There are many, many things I can do to reduce, I'm learning. Instead of buying canned beans, I can buy dried, for example. In

2001, enough steel cans were recycled to stretch from here to the moon and back three times. But these facilities use energy to recycle; I should concentrate on reducing. Instead of buying a twelve-pack of beer, I could ride my bike over to the brewpub and fill up a reusable growler. I could just cut back on beer, but that's another project entirely.

I fear hypocrisy; preaching vegans wearing leather shoes, and eco-love bumper stickers on fume-spewing junkers make me want to hide under a rock. Once I know that saving one glass bottle saves enough energy to light a one-hundred-watt bulb for four hours, that recycling a stack of newspapers six feet high can save one thirty-five-foot tree, that every Sunday in America we throw away 90 percent of newspapers—wasting *five hundred thousand trees*—I am a changed person. But I don't want to do anything halfway. If driving my recycling over to the dump once a week is causing unnecessary environmental damage, then I should simply *not use so much*.

It takes me only a day—less than a day, maybe—to understand why *Reduce* is the first word in the mantra *Reduce, Reuse, Recycle*. Considering my personal energy expenditure alone, I'm dizzied by the prospect of how much effort it will take to categorize and transport all of the waste I produce to recycling centers. But what of the energy the facilities use to process these containers and wrappers and other cluttering husks? Immediately, I am horrified by things like my bottle of mouthwash; who had the bright idea of selling people a big plastic bottle of liquid whose only purpose is to be spit out? It's brilliant, really. What of my *National Geographic*, wrapped in plastic with a paper sheet of some sort of useless information and chock-full of heavy paper encouragements to subscribe again or to give gift subscriptions? If anyone, I'd think, *National Geographic* should be encouraging people to share subscriptions rather than buy more. But let's be real, here.

I was in Nepal a few years ago and needed some sort of hygienic product (I can't remember which one), and I went to this

Recycling a stack of newspapers six feet high can save one thirty-five-foot tree . . . every Sunday in America we throw away 90 percent of newspapers—wasting five hundred thousand trees.

corner store–type place, not so much bigger than a carnival booth. It wasn't even something a person could walk through; there was a counter and an attendant, and available items were displayed on the shelves. One type each of whatever they sold. I said what I wanted, the guy handed it to me, and I gave him some rupees. Back home, I went to Walmart, and I remember standing in front of the cough drops for many minutes. *How many types of cough drops do we really need?* Look at the aisle of toilet paper. What types of beings are we that we have to choose from fifty types of tissue to wipe our backsides? I am frightened to know that I have spent many years wallowing in this way of living. I am also frightened by the awareness that it is so, so easy. So easy to buy this cheap, colorful crap and throw away the wrappers and eventually throw away the goods. I know a lot about immediate gratification. I know exactly what it feels like to feel empty in some way, and to pur-chase something shiny, or to drink or smoke something numbing, to try and fill that empty space.

What is it about our culture that is so empty that we're con-suming at such a rampant speed? What is this emptiness all about?

When I go to the recycling center for the first time with all my accrued recyclables, it's a cold, rainy Tuesday. It reminds me of winters in Eugene, Oregon. Nothing is pleasant about remem-bering winters in Eugene. *Rain is good, rain is good, rain is good,* I remind myself, especially here in Colorado, but cold wet seeps into my psyche, and as I sit in traffic listening to my windshield wipers thwack and slap, I find nothing as mournful as the reflection of tail lights on wet pavement.

It takes me three trips out to my car to load up my recycling—three trips carrying things that would have, last month, been dumped on the landfill. Bottles and cans, cardboard boxes, newspaper—I find appropriate receptacles for all these things, sharing grimaces with the other brave eco-conscious souls buffeted by wet gusts of wind. I feel somewhat like a poseur, though. They've got systems down; already everything is separated into well-used containers in their vehicles—they've been doing this a while. I'm wandering around squinting through the rain at the lists posted on the sides of the bins, a Wheat Thins box in one hand, an empty wine bottle under my arm, and a bag of empty cans in the other hand. I'm left with two empty oil quarts, an empty bottle of fuel-line cleaner, an Earth-Link CD, a jar of used paint thinner, and a broken pane of glass from a picture frame. I'm guessing they'll probably still be in my car when the apocalypse rolls around.

My next stop is Sunflower Market, and of course I forgot my knit grocery bag. How could I have this whole recycling thing planned out and forget my grocery bag? I have my school backpack in the car, so I bring it in. The tomatoes on sale come in nonrecyclable plastic containers. I put my pears into a plastic baggie without thinking. Being aware is something I really need to work on. I look wistfully at the string cheese. I like playing with my food; string cheese has always fulfilled my requirements of being nutritious, delicious, and entertaining. But all of those wrappers . . . I sigh and move on. There's a display of yoga accessories by the bulk food. A brick-type thing made of cork catches my eye. *Eco-Conscious Cork Yoga Brick,* it says on the cardboard advertising belt around the thing. *Achieve a deeper stretch with a brick made from all natural, sustainable, eco-friendly cork that provides superior comfort, traction, and support.* Give me a break, people. Contort on your phone book.

At the checkout, I cram wet celery, a dozen eggs, the tomatoes, pears, and a couple of cucumbers into my backpack with my notebook, not feeling entirely successful about the endeavor.

But when I go home, I rally: my garbage can is still only half full. I open it to dump in coffee grounds (reusable mesh filter, thankyouverymuch), and the whiff of deliquescing carrot peels, pear cores, and cucumber butts makes me reel. Evocative of . . . what? Of my father's garden at home; specifically, the compost pile. I'd like to say I clapped and exclaimed happily about another opportunity to shine my eco-love light, but in reality I sighed. I'm kind of starting to get on my own nerves with this militant determination to do every damned thing I can. It's really just not *like* me to be so adamant about doing the right thing all the time.

But this is the new me, right? I drive over to the Gardens on Spring Creek, a community garden in the middle of town, to see if they have a community compost pile. Turns out, oddly enough, they don't want my vegetarian offal. The woman there suggests that I start a worm-composting bin, and tells me I could keep the thing right under my sink. I'm still trying to wrap my mind around that idea.

I have to keep myself somewhere between feeling an increasing sense of eco-guilt as I learn about the ways I affect the environment, and feeling like I'm living on a moral high ground as I make some eco-friendly decisions in my life. The Hilda voice is necessary to snap us out of those sanctimonious hazes, but it would be great if that voice could be switched on and off. On, say, at the grocery store as we choose what we purchase, and on when we hold something empty in our hands and choose what to do with it, but then maybe off while we're enjoying ourselves on the beautiful earth we're helping to keep that way.

Bin Diver

CHRISTOPHER BUCKLEY

Christopher Buckley was born in California and grew up in Santa
Barbara during the 1950s and 1960s, where, as a kid, he'd walk
the creek down to the beach and squeeze through the culvert and
into the great cement tunnel that ran underneath the 101 Free-
way. Back then, smog was confined to the L.A. basin; the beaches
were unpolluted; and the ocean was clear, blue-green as glass.
There was no sprawl, urban or otherwise. There was plenty of
room for everyone, it then seemed. He started writing seriously in
1972, receiving his MA degree in 1974 from San Diego State University and an MFA degree from the University of California in 1976.
He is the author of fifteen books of poetry, two books of creative
nonfiction, and several edited anthologies of poetry and critical
books on poets. He's still trying to recapture the lost Eden of his
childhood, trying to preserve and cherish what he can of the
earth he knows and remembers.

bin diver [British] *n* **:** one who scavenges and extracts items cast
off in "bins." "Bin" translates into American as "garbage can,"
"Dumpster," etc. But the term "bin diver" has greater latitude and

includes anyone who collects discarded material, items that need not actually be in a bin or Dumpster, items that simply may have been left in the street or on the curb for one of those "big trash day" collections, or items just abandoned in a lot, lost, or dropped.

My wife, Nadya, is an artist. Anyone who knows artists knows they are inveterate collectors—feathers, bones, rocks, rags, bottles, labels and poster pieces, plastic toy figures, a piece of copper on the beach with a green patina, hinges, nails. If it looks like something, it might be useful for something.

Nadya is British. In England, bin diving is a half-honorable profession—usually it falls under the purview of the trash collectors who claim rights to anything thrown away in the bins or cast off along the curb on their routes, and some do a fair side business fixing up and/or selling what they turn up on their regular rounds. Lord help the individual whom official rubbish collectors find poaching a lamp or old chair from a bin on their patch.

My wife is a bin diver. We hardly go anywhere without picking up some bit of this or that—a walk around the neighborhood, a shopping trip downtown, a hike in the hills, a trip to a foreign country. We live by the beach and never go there without returning with several large stones or a backpack of smooth, thin stones, pieces of Pismo clam shells, and the rare unbroken sand dollar. Everywhere and at all times there is stuff someone no longer wants, or bits the sea or wind casts up, and we can have it just for the trouble of picking it up and hauling it away—stuff my wife is determined to use in one way or another and hence recycle.

As a kid in the 1950s, I loved a new toy as much as the next kid, but they were few and far between. Most of the things we used we made ourselves, picked up, or put together from what was at hand. We made pirate swords from the bark of palm trees, and one of our richest sources for material was one of the many new houses always being built nearby. We raided the scrap heap of ends and elbows of wood the carpenters threw away and used the bits of wood to build small houses and smooth out mud roads for our one or two Match Box metal cars.

My wife also knew this impulse. She grew up in England in the 1940s as the war ended. Children had to use their imaginations, or they found nothing with which to play. At her grandparents' cottage in Polruan, Cornwall, she and her friends would comb the beaches for whatever washed up. Her grandparents' cottage opened right on the lane, but there was a low cement wall separating the lane from the house, and on that shelf in the summers they would arrange their found treasures in a child's flea market. Blue and white bits of willow pattern plates, a teacup handle, blurry pieces of beach glass, fishing weights and hooks, or an unusual shell would be displayed, each with a price tag of a penny or tuppence; occasionally, anything exciting such as an earring, a button, or a small, blue medicine bottle would be marked six pence. The world was not awash in plastic then, and although she never remembers selling anything to the tourists and passersby, she recalls many an afternoon's entertainment arranging their finds and cataloging treasure. The discards of the world were put to use in the hands of children, and so her gleaning and bin-giving habits developed early.

It takes dedication and a good eye—often as not the artist's eye—to notice a bit of unwanted furniture, piece of broken tile, or bent tin frame and know that with some rudimentary attention, it can recapture some little light from your past. My wife is a talented artist, and a talented bin diver. She has furnished half our house, or more, with bookshelves; metal patio tables; coffee tables; matching midcentury modern armchairs; tables, desks, and chests of drawers; metal standing lamps from streets in Hoboken and Athens, Ohio; and matching bed stand china lamps in the shape of horse heads— all picked up off the curb or in the alley on a big trash day, or snatched up on arrival at her favorite thrift shop. And at the top of this heap are two matching art deco bedside tables. These were rescued from a proverbially dank basement in a university where we both used to teach, a dark room where art students and the janitorial staff used to kill time smoking and more than likely covertly taking "a wee drop of the creature" as Bing put it in *Going My Way*. The paint was peeling, and there were finger-long black cigarette burns on the top, but with sanding, primer, and a double coat of period leather-orange paint, they gleamed like a thousand-dollar set from an antique shop, which is just what they are, thanks to her keen eye and restoration.

Sanding, staining, rewiring, fitting a new shade, finding new glass, applying a little paint, or sometimes leaving as is and placing just so in the garden against some driftwood hauled back from the beach, and voila! You spend some energy, save some money, and do your little bit to oppose conspicuous consumption and the use-once-and-toss society—whose habits with disposable goods, it can be argued, are deleterious to character and social consciousness as well as the planet we are poisoning. Witness the junk pool that is now the Mediterranean—awash with Styrofoam, cling wrap, water bottles, Frisbees, cups, detergent bottles, to just get started. I remember, in 1984, standing on the deck of a ferryboat returning to Piraeus from Santorini and watching a crewman simply sweep all the bottles, bags, coffee cups, paper plates, and other trash over the side into the sea just before they put into harbor to pick up the next load of tourists. And a few weeks ago, I was talking to a friend who was fishing fifteen miles off the coast of Costa Rica on vacation when he saw a refrigerator go floating by their boat.

Back home, we have friends with rooms full of new furniture bought at some big chain showroom, furniture so stiff and angular, so very emerald green, or mulberry, so very clean from the fact that the rooms in which it is placed are rarely used. They remarked that our furniture looked like it was leftover from grad school. What, we wondered, was wrong with that? We like an object with character, gravity, history, and made the old way with the weight of real wood—natural colors and a few scars and scrapes adding character. The county landfill nearby now has separate piles for metal, wood, TVs, and computers—pyramids of toxic discards twenty or thirty feet high, and more coming every day. Average life of a computer? Three years tops for most people. Now, even most thrift stores will not take them as donations. We at least are not contributing as much as most to a landfill that will soon be filled up. Then what? The value of a piece is in its construction and function, whether it's a hall table or some Moorish tiles worn rough by the elements and rescued from a discard heap by a lighthouse.

We were in Menorca on my first sabbatical after twenty years of work. We were living on less than half pay. Both my wife and I had some health problems at that time, and mentally, psychically, I could feel the flames at my heels. I realized I had been spending far too much time rearranging the names on my list of colleagues for the top floor in the hotel fire. We took the full year, the diminished pay, so we might stare into the reasonable silence and the blue and recover there along the sea. Nadya had a British friend with a flat in Menorca that was not rented for the winter, which was the off-season. She let us have it for a little over three hundred dollars a month, sparsely furnished. We were well prepared to make do once on the island.

   One of the first things we noticed on our walks around Es Castell, on the easternmost tip of the island, was that on varying days at varying places along the sidewalks, piles of discarded furniture and household items would appear—everything from beds and wardrobes and chairs to a small wood chest with fishing line and hooks. The first week there we came across a pile of discards outside a bar that had closed down. Nadya did not even look around before selecting some wicker chairs, a wobbly olivewood entry-hall table with woodworm, and a broken milking stool, which we would carry back to our flat and use and admire. I turned up a hat rack fashioned from hand-twisted wire. Both the entry-hall table and the hat rack are in our home today.

   Also, we collected tiles, a dozen or so inlaid with Moorish designs in a dull red and gold, which had been dumped in back of a lighthouse up the coast from Es Castell. Nadya integrated them into a brick patio she hand laid in our house. She also collected handmade tiles from walls and kitchens in derelict houses in and around Mahon, the capital. These were low-fired tiles, and, once she had them, she glued pieces back together and repainted the original pattern of olive leaves across them.

On one of these discard heaps on the street, there was a large chest of drawers, which, although damaged, still had its brass hardware intact. Nadya removed the keyhole lock plate and some handles and brought them back to repair her friend's pine wardrobe in the flat. Oh, the lovely little wood chest with the fishing gear—we picked that up off a pile as the chest was very well-made and in good condition. But what would we do with all of the line and hooks? We always said hello to the local ragman, an old gent in a sea captain's hat who pushed a cart about picking up what he could—a nice local who always tipped his cap to us, possibly out of professional courtesy. I saw him returning to his home for siesta. I went back and collected the chest and left it by his door during the shady, sleepy hours of the day when no one would see me. The next morning, the chest was gone, and so put to good use I was sure.

Christmas came and there were few trees for sale on the island—expensive to ship in and not really part of the tradition. The Spanish celebrate the Feast of the Kings/the Epiphany twelve days after Christmas itself. There were no big sales, no push to buy and exchange presents. The handful of Christmas trees we did see for sale we could not afford. So we picked up a dry bush, a large tumbleweed really, which had been polished by the wind and salt. It was about three feet tall, and we set it up on a bin-dived table in the living room of the flat. We collected eucalyptus pods and painted them silver and gold and hung them with green thread on the "tree." We found small pine cones and hung them with red ribbon and cut several snowflakes from my typing paper and hung them as well. Everything we needed turned up along the road, and we still think it was our best Christmas yet.

Writer friends from California came for a January visit. Jon was an old poetry pal of mine, and his wife, Dixie, was, among many things, a poet, novelist, painter, and photographer. One afternoon after one of the cheap and wonderful local menu del dia lunches, we drove a rented car to a beach on the north side of the island to take a walk along the shore. Washed up all over the beach like seaweed was a ton of plastic: kids' action figures, plastic soldiers, Disney characters, nylon chord, flip flops (never a pair), plastic caps, pill boxes, water bottles, laundry and dish detergent containers, balls, buckets and spades, every bit and bob imaginable. Dixie began to collect and arrange and photograph. Jon and Nadya and I hauled in every bit of plastic we could from the shoreline, and Dixie arranged collages and snapped pictures. While there was no other real use for all of this beyond a photo collage, we at least got a great deal of it off the beach.

On a last day of Jon and Dixie's visit, Dixie and Nadya wanted to drive out to the dump and look around. Jon and I were not enthusiastic, knowing that they'd come up with more stuff to cart back. Nonetheless, we drove out, and the dump was deserted. Predictably, Dixie and Nadya were out of the car and immediately on top of a heap of jars and bottles. Nadya soon returned with an empty gin bottle; the label read "Xorigur," a north African word that the local language, Menorquí (which is an adaptation of Catalan), absorbed long ago. This bottle was forty or fifty years old, made from a mold. Pressed into the glass near the top, in lieu of a label, was "GIN XORIGUER ★ MAHON." The letters were set deeply into the glass. Somewhere back in the day, bottle makers poured glass by hand into a mold, no computer-monitored machines metering out the textured green glass. Thickly poured and pressed in this old fashioned shape and size, this was a bottle that you could well imagine in the hand of Stephano or Trinculo, washed up on Prospero's island.

While poking around in a broken bus, I discovered a small metal tag behind the driver's seat reading, "NO HABLAR CON EL

While poking around in a broken bus.

CONDUCTOR" on a deep blue tin strip printed and outlined in silver. I pried it off and pointed out the relative weight of what I had collected compared to what Nadya and Dixie had accumulated. Nadya's point was that all of her found items would be used in the house or in art projects. Mine—well, I prized it for its ironic declaration; no one I know has ever spoken with "the Conductor," and I do not trust those who proclaim that they have. This tag to my mind represented our relation to the maker, the metaphysical construct if there were one.

Correct or incorrect as that might be, we have nonetheless, it seems clear, at least a responsibility to ourselves if not to those who follow us—if not some perhaps spiritual obligation—to recycle what little we can, to avoid wasting even the least bit given to us, in wealth or in relative poverty, to be resourceful stewards of the planet.

Why I Love the Dump

CHAVAWN KELLEY

Chavawn Kelley's work has appeared in *Quarterly West, Northern Lights, Creative Nonfiction,* and *Hayden's Ferry Review* and has been nominated for the Pushcart Prize and cited in the *Best American Essays* series. She is the recipient of fellowships from the Wyoming Arts Council and the Ucross Foundation. Of this piece, she says, "The dump represents a landscape of options thought to be exhausted, a place where the consequences of our actions are laid out before us."

In our small Wyoming town, we haul our own garbage to the dump—there is no public trash service. My husband and I put our garbage in paper bags, and when one is full, we close it and staple it shut. Stapled is better since we store the bags for a while on the back porch and since I'm just compulsive enough that I don't want my business to blow away and become everybody else's business. When it's time, we load the truck and make a dump run. In the summer, the garbage asserts with aromatic authority "when it's

The dump is our midden, our pile of oyster shells by the estuary. It is the green and lilac bottles a good arm's throw behind the miner's shack. It is the pottery shards on top of the mesa.

time." But in the winter on the unheated back porch, our bags multiply contentedly until we're ready to take them.

Usually, I drive Junior, our Jeep pickup, the couple of blocks to Main Street. I turn east, cross the river, then go north on Highway 789. Climbing out of the valley, Junior and I pass the tree-lined grounds of the State Training School for the disadvantaged. Then we blow past a band of dirty sheep by a wallow. From their scrap of shrub, all is faded sandstone. We turn right onto the dump road.

The narrow blacktop crosses a bare expanse, carries us up a grade, and spills us out. Lurching from the pavement, we enter the dumping ground. Between the "Dump Here" signs, we find the site. It's never where you left it; it progresses by degrees like the shadow on a sundial. I back in beside my neighbors. Seagulls buzz overhead. Down the line, pickups are parked with their tailgates hanging out. Some folks say hi and some avert their eyes, and everyone shovels his or her dejecture in with everyone else's. A Caterpillar scrapes a little earth over it.

Everyone should have this privilege. The dump is our midden, our pile of oyster shells by the estuary. It is the green and lilac bottles a good arm's throw behind the miner's shack. It is the pottery shards on top of the mesa. *Our* dump is grocery sacks and grass clippings in the dun-colored dust of summer. Crunchy elk carcasses in the lingering heat of fall. Christmas trees thrown out with the crush of winter's Yuletide. And my favorite, the plunder left from the purge that is triggered by the first push of a tulip.

There is no charge at the dump—not to the souls depositing the remains of their spent riches, nor to the foragers who find further value. Our dump is not a dimple or a pit. Mostly it is a slope, and we leave our offering at the base or heave it to the top.

One spring day, a day so clean it hurt, I looked out after pitching my brown paper bags. In that pure and undiffused light, every ordinary object cut with the sharpness that only comes after a good rain. The sky overarched the valley, and across the valley the Wind River Mountains rose like a higher, unbalanced reflection of the garbage mound I stood before, helping to build. The clarity of the message dazzled me: with modern garbage, there is no "away."

It's a perverted cycle. Nothing breaks down here. It just builds up.

Just as the grocery store saves us from knowing where our food comes from, Throwing It Away gives us the freedom of not knowing where our household rubbish goes. In municipalities across the United States, we throw our garbage away only about as far as the curb. Then it becomes the business of Garbage Collection. When I take my garbage to the dump, I know where it goes, and the dogs don't knock it over.

When we tried to leave, the Jeep had to work to get us out. Thick mud tugged at the tires and was thrown against the wheel wells. *Whoomph, whoomph, whoomph,* we set tracks back toward town.

When camping in bear country, garbage can be costly. Every night after dinner, my friends and I load our food and garbage into two nylon zip bags. We load the stove and the nylon wind pants we wore to cook in. When we're finished brushing our teeth, we load our toothbrushes and our toothpaste, too. The bears we're avoiding are born scavengers, attracted by smell. We zip our bags closed and suspend them from a highline strung between tall Engelmann spruce and whitebark pines. Every morning, one of us makes the frosty trek to the hang site to haul the bags—yet again untouched by our unseen threat—to a suitable kitchen site on the streambed. Downwind.

The packs we carry in the backcountry are heavy. We rely on our physical strength, but in a larger sense, we are unencumbered. Life is reduced to the elemental. Cooking and eating, clothing, shelter, and hygiene. Self-preservation and group safety.

On the first night of one particular trip, where the Wiggins Fork was still wide and its bank was wide and sandy, we acted out bear encounters. To play the bear, we pointed knuckles back for ears and rushed with a ferocious charge. The human backed away slowly, and without looking the bear eye-to-eye, spoke up with as much composure as possible: "Sorry. Didn't mean to walk up on you. Please don't eat me!"

Later, when no one was around, I felt an animal stir, but it was me. I took off my shoes and drew alternating half circles in the sand with my left and right toes: *ronds de jambe à terre*. Secretly, I continued with *grand battements, arabesques,* and *attitude*. The movements that eluded me as a child during Saturday morning classes came easily here. I sprang like a cat, *pas de chat*, and jumped with the broad leaps of a stag. Arms and legs everywhere, I twirled and danced. My heart beat *allegro*.

Yellowstone Lake was blasted out around five million years ago. Most of Yellowstone's hot-boweled volcanoes had already blown themselves to bits forty-five million years earlier, dumping truckloads of ash, covering thousands of square miles. Working on the mess, the wind blew and the water scoured. After little more than an overnight (in geological terms) and not far from my house (in Wyoming terms), the sun climbed the remaining heap, and the Absaroka Range came to light. The charcoal-colored walls resemble dull, crinkled foil, and the peaks pick and jag at the sky. The runoff makes its way down in an endless tumble over rocks cemented in clumps like colored eggs in putty.

In the Absarokas, bear scat is of great fascination. The pass was littered with it, and we inspected every clump, trying to determine if it was from a black bear or a grizzly. Hard to know, but while traveling we are ever mindful of whose range we tread upon. Earlier, on the trail, we had collected to peer into a puddle, through gray water like a mirror with its silver worn away. We strained as if to see into some metaphysical parallel world. Below the reflections of our four faces, we barely made out a single faint track laid days ago. Or maybe that's what we thought we saw. What did we hope to learn?

After dinner, we migrated with our bags up from Bear Creek's boulders and the noisy water into the woods and hung the food. We'd perched our blue rainfly on a broad bench on the mountainside. Andre and Andy sat on the hill to talk, and Ashley moved farther up to write. The men's murmuring mixed with the water's, and I laid out a sleeping pad in the refrigerated air and sat with my legs stretched long. I was warm in my fleecy fabrics, thick socks, mittens, and hat.

A high barking screeched from down the valley, and I looked up. In the bruised light, I squinted as though through the pinhole of a diorama. I watched a wave of elk wash up onto the opposite hill and run back down again and again. If they thought of it as dancing, then they were. They drank from the mouth of the tiny tributary from which I'd bathed. They moved toward me, but their forms grew dimmer in the fading light. Finally, they flew up the mountainside and disappeared. I drew breath and realized I'd begun to shiver.

Ursus arctos horribilis once set track across much of North America, including the more temperate lowlands. We *Homo sapiens* moved where we could make a passable living, and the nature of our activities was such that the two ranges could not be reconciled. The grizzly retreated to the heights, and now the Wilderness Act says that I am a visitor who cannot remain here. That's the price. There was a time when, down lower, it was the bear who did not remain. That price: a scaled-down population of *Ursus arctos horribilis* now patrols a puny 1 percent of its original territory.

In two days we'll be picked up near the Forest Service guard station on the East Fork of the Wind River. It'll feel good to be home. It's not easy to make a living in the small town where I live, though. Geography and isolation limit the economy. Or at least that's how it's been. But the geography holds an attraction. For now, at least, we're pretty small in number and income. Which is why we can afford to keep a fairly small public dump.

When I get home, I'll go there to dispose of the garbage from our trip. How peculiar to haul it out of one place just to throw it away in another, but we did, after all, haul it up here. The separation may be unnatural, but I'm glad for places where our nature is restrained. And our economy is restrained even further. In these places, I can be a moth, the color of glacier ice, lighting on a rock. Or examine how on earth I can imagine myself to be such a moth. Our garbage mound may never become a mountain range overtaking the Wind Rivers or the Absarokas, but I feel certain that as the one grows, the others are diminished.

On our last morning in the mountains, I grab the metal trowel that is central to our experience and start on a short walk. I should be talking out loud or singing so that no bear is startled on her daily rounds. Instead, I make my way quietly. After I've gone far enough, I find a semiflat, open spot under a tree, and I etch out a square slightly bigger than my fist. I slip the trowel blade under the duff, loosen it, and lift it out. I set it aside and dig deeper into the young mountain soil. When my cathole is about a fist deep, I uncinch my pants and push the layers down. I park and look over the valley with my tailgate hanging out.

I drop my dirtied fir cones into the hole with my waste. I pull up my cotton drawers, my long underwear, and my wind pants, and I replace the square of duff and stir the needles to erase the edges. Everyone should have this privilege.

The Turf, the Game, and the Radio

JULIANNE COUCH

Julianne Couch is the author of *Jukeboxes & Jackalopes: A Wyoming Bar Journey*. Her essays have appeared in *High Country News, Owen Wister Review, Heritage of the Great Plains, Hard Ground: Writing the Rockies, Ahead of Their Time: Wyoming Voices for the Wilderness,* and other publications. She watches students, athletes, and coaches circulate—and pollution and population levels elevate—from her home in Laramie, Wyoming. She teaches in the English Department at the University of Wyoming.

One warm and windy summer afternoon a few years ago, my husband, Ron, and I rode our bicycles across Laramie for a Colts baseball game. The University of Wyoming once had its own team, but the sport was discontinued in the mid-1990s. That left a very nice baseball field mostly empty for kids' leagues and the occasional lost moose or deer that'd wandered in from the mountains and become disoriented by the fence. On the afternoon in question, we were going to see Laramie's team in the inaugural season of the Mountain Collegiate Baseball League. We welcomed the return of real baseball, even though it wasn't a regular university team. Instead, each summer we'd have a different group of college all-star league players here from all over the country.

We could bike to the baseball field from our home in five or ten minutes, depending on the direction of the wind. Both our bicycles are relics: Ron's is a ten-speed with skinny tires and sand-brown paint abandoned by the occupants of a house we once lived in; mine is a purple Schwinn Western Flyer given me for my thirtieth birthday, now more years ago than I care to count. One year, Ron surprised me by mounting a small wicker basket between the front handles and later added a little bell I could *br-ring* in self-defense whenever one of Laramie's reckless college-student drivers swerved too close, cell phone planted in ear.

Our ride home from seeing the Colts win the game took us past War Memorial Stadium, home of the University of Wyoming Cowboy football team. The fifty-plus-year-old stadium was undergoing major renovation to the field and stands alike, thanks to significant funding from the state legislature and some wealthy Wyoming oil entrepreneurs.

The donors themselves, the Mick and Susie McMurry family and the John and Mari Ann Martin family, own a large interest in one of the richest and most active natural gas fields in the state. Jonah Field was once just the name of twenty-one thousand acres of prairie about thirty miles south of Pinedale, in the Upper Green River valley. On the surface, it is a typical patch of Wyoming rangeland, home to the usual mobs of pronghorn antelope and sage grouse. But just under the sagebrush and sand is trapped 10.5 trillion cubic feet of natural gas. That gas is being pumped out now with the efficiency of a well-schooled West Coast offense, making lots of money for the McMurrys, Martins, and others. Thus, the donation to the university's athletic program. In their honor, the football field is now called "Jonah Field." "Jonah Field Field" would have been redundant.

To make room for Jonah Field's fancy new artificial turf, the old grass had to be removed. The university advertised in our local paper, the *Boomerang*, that chunks of the old grass would be available to anyone who wanted them, whether for practical or sentimental reasons. The turf was cut up and carted away by Laramie locals. One neighbor up the road from us created a rock garden in the strip of land between the sidewalk and the street. Amongst the small pebbles of the rock garden now straddles a large "W" for Wyoming, created from the repurposed turf of the former Cowboy Field.

After the old turf found new homes, it was time for the Jonah Field field to be born. The new playing surface, called the "Desso Challenge Pro 60 Monofilament Synthetic Turf System," is constructed of artificial grass fibers specifically developed for football. The turf was developed by DESSO DLW Sports Systems of Dendermonde, Belgium. It was installed by workers from an outfit in Colorado, who had been hard at work on the day we pedaled home from the baseball game.

Ron and I were eager to see the progress at the stadium. The workers must have knocked off early on that day, because as we rode by to take a closer look at their handiwork, no workers were to be seen. The stadium gates were wide open, but the field was deserted. That might be an unheard of state of affairs in other places, but in Laramie, where virtually no one locks the doors to anything, it was par for the course.

Ron and I pulled in to the stadium and got off our bicycles. We stealthily approached the field, thinking at any moment the PA system would boom with a directive that we should stop where we were and get our butts back on our bikes. It would have felt like trespassing to go clear out onto the virgin turf that would soon support the heroic football deeds of our star players such as quarterback Corey Bramlet and wide receiver Jovon Bouknight. But we had to approach at least close enough to dip our fingers into the south end zone and swoosh our bare toes over the artificial grass fibers.

As a natural-grass reactionary, even I had to admit that this new surface was spectacular. The fibers were long and lush. The color was green—paint-chip green, crayon green, not Laramie high-desert-drought green. The white yard markers and hash marks had a vibrant permanence no mere paint could match. The word "Wyoming" in gold-on-brown fibers in one end zone and "Cowboys" in the other would never fade no matter how many touchdowns and touchdown dances were executed by the home team and visitors.

We resisted the urge to strip off and roll naked on the Cowboy's bucking horse and rider logo at the fifty-yard line. But we couldn't resist the sight of a brimming, unguarded industrial-sized Dumpster, teeming with trim remnants of the Desso Challenge Pro 60 Monofilament Synthetic Turf System.

We stood on tiptoes on the rungs of the Dumpter's metal ladder, peering in at the discarded turf strips. The first piece we saw that we could reach without descending into the mess was about six inches wide but appeared to be the width of the end zone. Another was tangled in a long, gluey, unusable heap. But a third discarded strip was about four inches wide and maybe ten feet long. Perfect. For what purpose, we didn't care. All we knew was that it met our first criterion: it would fit into the wicker basket of my Schwinn Western Flyer.

We moved with the speed of the paranoid—casual yet clumsy-fast. We dragged the piece that struck our fancy out of the Dumpster and laid it out on the ground, like a freshly caught trout on the bank of a stream. Ron hadn't thought to carry his almost always-present pocketknife to the baseball game, so we had to take the piece all or nothing. He stood on one end and I on the other, as if we were about to shake out a laundered sheet. Then he, with hands strengthened from years of squeezing sleeping bag pads into tight cylinders, rolled and crammed the bright green remnant of the Synthetic Turf System into a tubular ball.

This was one day I wish we'd driven or walked to the baseball game, as we sometimes did. Instead, we had my purple bike with fat tires and undersized basket to transport our new treasure. Into the basket went the ball of turf, which must have weighed ten pounds. We remounted our bikes: Ron, pedaling with ease in the twenty-mile-per-hour breeze of a Laramie afternoon; I, struggling to propel myself forward in a fairly straight line, fighting with the extra weight. The ball of turf shoved the basket down so that it threatened to rub against the front tire. I managed to hold the handlebars steady, even as we bounced along the game-trail-like footpath across LaPrele Park, past the antelope that drink from the creek that feeds the park's fishing pond. I pumped with my waning breaths and made it up the final steep hill to home. We unfurled the turf ball on the edge of the deck and, in our imaginations, tried it out in several possible locations: as doormat, as garden border, as habitat for the resin raccoon and gnome.

There had been no question of leaving the remnant behind in the Dumpster. The new turf symbolized one of the things I'd come to love about Wyoming. There are so few of us living here, and so few fragments of shared culture, that college athletics, which never appealed to me in the large midwestern city where I grew up, had become over the years more than a passion. I was obsessed with the Wyoming Cowboys men's basketball and football teams.

I went to some games, but mostly I listened on the radio. Sometimes I did both at the same time. Occasionally, I listened to the radio while watching a rare broadcast of Wyoming athletics on television, TV announcers muted. I'd become mesmerized by Dave Walsh, the "Voice of the Cowboys" and his broadcast partner and color analyst, Kevin McKinney. In the beginning, I didn't care that much about the games; I just wanted to hear what they said about them: Dave, with his uncanny play-by-play and understated humor, and Kevin with his journalistic integrity in spite of his "brown-and-gold eyes." Both of them made the games worth listening to even on those occasions when the teams went down in devastating defeat.

Each fall, during the early years of my Cowboys obsession, Ron and I would get a permit and go to the Snowy Range Mountains to cut dead trees for firewood. We'd drive the pickup truck down two-tracks deep into the forest. We'd find a dead tree and zip it down with a chainsaw, careful to keep a watchful eye on our dogs, one brown and one gold, who were barking and bounding without a care among the trees. Over the din, we could hear the truck's AM radio picking up KOWB's broadcast of the Cowboy's football game. After the chainsaw and dog din was stilled, we'd sit on a log sipping a cold Miller Genuine Draft beer and tossing pretzels to the dogs and gray jays. We'd listen to Dave and Kevin describe goal-line stands, fantastic catch-and-runs, or miraculous interceptions by our wicked-fast defense. As we loaded the firewood into the truck and headed down the mountain and across the valley toward home, we'd hear Dave and Kevin deadpan about the twenty-three-year-old sophomore quarterback of the Brigham Young University Cougars, one of Wyoming's perennial sports enemies whose players were always several years older than our own. Dave: "And here's the twenty-three-year old quarterback." Kevin: "Isn't he a sophomore?" Dave: "Let's see . . . yes, that's what it says here in the media guide. Sophomore." Our quarterback at the time, I recall, was a twenty-two-year-old senior.

After fall football season ended and the firewood was stacked for burning, it was time for winter basketball. Mostly we'd listen to basketball games at home, snug in front of a crackling fire, mugs of tea in our hands and dogs asleep at our feet. When we went to the games in person, we'd bring radios with headphones so we could listen to KOWB. We'd purchased two yellow M&M character radios at the Laramie Radio Shack on sale, for $4.99 each. Ron took the legs off his so it could be tucked unobtrusively into his pocket. I waved mine proudly in my hand as I cheered on the Cowboys. We named the radios Dave and Kevin.

The radios were a few years old but still in fine voice the fall of the first football season to be played on the new Jonah Field. It was a warm day in September, and Ron and I rode our trusty bicycles to the game. From our seats high up in the stadium, we could look out over the top of the opposite bleachers and see the Snowy Range, dark with pine forest. Far below us, the new turf gleamed like a magic carpet. The jewel-green grass, the bright white yard markers, the glorious brown-and-gold end zones were a quilt against which gleamed the Western Thunder Marching Band in their tall, tasseled hats. The school fight song, "Ragtime Cowboy Joe," rang clear and loud in the oval stadium, buoyed by the acoustics-loving turf. The Cowboys' opponent that day was Louisiana-Monroe. The Cowboys won, 38 to 0, and, as Dave and Kevin would say, all was well in 'Pokes Nation.

In the years since we listened to Dave and Kevin, we've seen more than just college student-athletes come and go from our lives. We've moved out of the house that had the wood-burning stove—the house where we found the bike that became Ron's—to our new house across the park at the top of the steep hill. Our brown and gold dogs are no longer living but are buried together in the back-yard of the new house. The pickup truck sits out front, with a quarter-million miles on its odometer and a for-sale sign in its window. We don't need so much firewood now. Our glass-doored fireplace in this house is more decorative than utilitarian, unlike the woodstove in the old house. The last time we needed firewood we bought half a cord from some folks who delivered it by dumping it into the alley behind our house, where we snugged it into neat rows against the fence. Later that winter, most of it was stolen and burned in a pyre after a particularly raucous football game against those BYU Cougars.

In spite of the changes, Dave and Kevin carry on as the Voice of the Wyoming Cowboys and broadcast partners. Our strip of Jonah Field is still balled up, nestled in the garage on top of the chest freezer among the boxes and bottles that await recycling. We are still trying to figure out the perfect use for the turf. Last summer we built a backyard shed with a little gravel pad at the entrance framed by landscape timbers. I'd like to take the turf trim and tack it down to the timbers to give it a fresh, Pleasantville look. Ron is still weighing the idea. In other words, he hasn't given in yet.

In the meantime, in the other Jonah Field, the one south of Pinedale, natural gas that has been under the surface for sixty-five million years is quickly being coaxed from its hidey holes. The

In the other Jonah Field, the one south of Pinedale, natural gas that has been under the surface for sixty-five million years is quickly being coaxed from its hidey holes. The wide open, pristine Wyoming countryside is changed forever by the unpleasant side effects of the energy boom that, admittedly, funds much of what we enjoy in our state.

wide open, pristine Wyoming countryside is changed forever by the unpleasant side effects of the energy boom that, admittedly, funds much of what we enjoy in our state. Pumps in this and other nearby fields run all day every day, and almost all year long. Roads to get workers back and forth to the well pads are plentiful to the point of redundancy, and their effect will be permanent. The pronghorn antelope have apparently found a way to ignore the noise and the traffic for now, but the long-term impact on their ancient migration route remains to be seen. The mule deer, elk, and other big game in the area also have a lot of change to cope with, and the sage grouse surely notice a crowd as they go about nesting, mating, and brooding each year. Whether they'll give up and go someplace else also remains to be seen. Whether there even is someplace to go remains to be seen, too.

Meanwhile, this winter in 'Pokes Nation, our Wyoming Cowboy basketball team's promising start to the season is fading away. After the season ends, Dave and Kevin—the radios—will go into the storage shed for the summer. Dave and Kevin—the people—will take a break and rest their voices. We'll ride our bicycles to see yet another incarnation of the Laramie Colts play baseball. We'll count the months until fall, when the Western Thunder Marching Band rolls across the Desso Challenge Pro 60 Monofilament Synthetic Turf System, and we all sing "Ragtime Cowboy Joe" together. The antelope that graze in our neighborhood park will hear the clamor. They'll lift their heads at the sound and wonder what the heck we have to cheer about.

It Keeps the Heart Happy

LAURA PRITCHETT

Laura Pritchett is the author of a novel, *Sky Bridge*, which won the WILLA Literary Award, and a collection of short stories, *Hell's Bottom, Colorado*, which won the PEN USA award and the Milkweed National Fiction Prize. Pritchett is coeditor of and contributor to two other books—*Home Land: Ranching and a West that Works* and *Pulse of the River: Colorado Writers Speak for the Endangered Cache la Poudre*. Pritchett's work has also appeared in numerous magazines, including *The Sun, Orion, High Desert Journal, High Country News,* and *5280*. She holds a PhD in literature from Purdue University. She lives in northern Colorado, near the small cattle ranch where she was raised.

"Dive, DIVE, DI——VE!" yips my friend Tim, and then he makes the sound of a submerging submarine: "eeeEEERR, eeEERRRR!" This, he follows with an address: "100 East Oak Street!"

I click down the phone, get in the car, and meet him at the given location. His message is code; there is a diving emergency— a Dumpster so good, so overflowing, so spectacular as to need both of our attentions. I leap out of the car and pull on my work gloves. He puts down a stepladder and heaves himself up. One treasure after another he hands me, and I stick them in his car. I stand at the edge of the Dumpster, giving him suggestions on where to probe or what sacks to rip open, and he pushes around the multitude of plastic trash sacks and cardboard boxes. Someone is clearly moving out today, and here come the trappings of an entire household. A huge ceramic piggybank! An oil-color painting in an oak frame! An iron skillet, bowling shoes, a box of jewelry, a tent! We giggle and scan the horizon for cops. Life is tremendous.

Tim is a geologist, or was, until he was stricken with a nervous system disorder that the doctors have been unable to identify or treat, other than to offer narcotics. He's too thin, and quite tall, with dark, slightly graying hair and the eyes of someone who has suffered chronic and unmitigated pain for more than ten years. He Dumpster dives frequently, generally in the mornings or evenings, and when I can—which is not as often as I like—I go with him. Sometimes it's just me; sometimes my two young children tag along.

Recently, he and I found, either separately or together, an air hockey table, a bag of pot, a stereo system, two houseplants, a toaster, a conch shell, a bong, a digital camera, an army jeep gas tank, two cell phones, a collapsible wheelchair, some new tools, and, well, a box of brand-new, still-packaged dildos. The Best Find of the Week prize recently went to Tim, who pulled out a crystal that had another crystal, called "rutile," growing in it; gold feathers inside purple quartz.

His house is stocked with things from Dumpsters—paintings, clothes, kitchen utensils, plants. The majority of my kids' toys and clothes are from Dumpsters. So are the shoes and jeans I'm wearing as I write this, and so, no doubt, are the clothes Tim is wearing at this very moment, at his home. We realize that this is socially weird, but we don't care. This Dumpster diving is a funny and strange bond that we share and cherish.

As far as I can tell, we dive for four reasons.

One is the environment. As a geologist and prospector, Tim knows, for example, how expensive aluminum is to mine from the earth—it comes from bauxite, and, while aluminum is the most common element in the earth's crust, it is also locked-in chemically and must be heated to enormous temperatures to get out, which takes an unbelievable amount of energy. Since I've been digging out beer cans from the Dumpster (that sits about two feet from a recycling area), I have learned things: that manufacturing aluminum cans out of recycled aluminum takes 95 percent less energy than aluminum obtained from bauxite, that about thirty aluminum cans are produced from one pound of aluminum, and that each aluminum can requires about three thousand British thermal units (Btus) to produce it. So, Tim calculates, doing some sort of mental mathematics foreign to me, every two or three cans we recycle (or pick from a Dumpster) basically saves a pound of coal.

He's telling me this because sometimes I get whiny. I'm here for the *treasures*. But no, Tim has a rule, which he insists on enforcing: that while seeking treasure, we take out the boring old recyclables too. We can't, of course, take out *everything*—otherwise, we'd spend the whole day emptying the Dumpsters of nearly all they contain. But we take out quite a lot.

Tim can't ignore this stuff, and I've come to understand why. He can see, in his mind's eye, what's really being thrown away—what the earth gave up for these materials. He sees what it really took to make that toaster oven or vacuum or pop can. He sees how our minerals are being depleted by a society that cannot learn to recycle or fix.

Considering how much pain this diving causes him because of his disorder—how much it hurts him to sometimes move his hands or his neck—it stabs my heart to know that what *he* expends is so much greater than the average able-bodied person. I see *him* the way he sees the earth's minerals. Here is a man who is being depleted by other's propensity for depleting the world.

I am always wishing: if only that person would have spent a few extra moments taking things to the recycling center, or to Goodwill—that they had one iota of the care he does. And he is always wishing: if only the earth did not have to give so much, if only we cared for it the way we should.

We have our wishes, for each other, for the world, and in our wishing, our bond to each other, and to the earth, tightens.

This is the real reason we dive, but a second reason is paramount too: the money. We have huge garage sales with all this stuff, and when people ask us, as they always do, "Wow, where'd you get all this stuff?" Tim gives his sly-but-true answer: "Oh, it's a multi-family garage sale." Tim lives on the garage sale income and disability checks, and though he lives in a beautiful small house in the old part of town, he lives modestly and sometimes confesses that if money weren't so tight, he could pay for thus-and-thus medication or treatment. I'm a writer—enough said—and the money I've earned from his last few garage sales has bought the time I've needed for my own writing projects instead of the for-hire writing jobs that I despise. Tim fixes and cleans everything, and though the buyers get good deals, when we count the money at the end of the day, the pay is pretty good.

A third reason we dive, Tim and I, is that we simply love to find things. It's good for our souls; seeking is ingrained deep in our bodies. We grew up in different states and are from different backgrounds, and we met well into adulthood, but we both share that joy that some people have about discovery—arrowheads, rocks, a coin on the sidewalk. It gives us a thrill; it makes our day.

The final reason is that we have fun. Unbelievable fun. My kids have come to regard Dumpster diving as one of the best possible ways to spend a Saturday, and when I'm feeling low, I call Tim up to see what he's found, or if he's in the mood to go. One late night, we were diving with another friend, Mike, with headlamps on and flashlights ready to wave away the raccoons that invariably share the Dumpsters with us. Mike pulled out an enormous bra—the biggest I have ever seen—and tilted his head at it in wonder. We all burst out in a genuine, hearty laugh, not at the woman who wore it, just at the oddness of it, the way the lacy cups hung from his hand in the moonlight.

But we discover heartbreak, too: Last month, Tim found a large tub of letters, the outside of the envelopes covered in such fancy, small script that he was intrigued enough to pull just one rubber-banded package out. We read some of the letters together, unraveling the story of a teenage boy put in jail for dealing drugs to support his girlfriend and their forthcoming child; this boy-man filled line after line of romantic babblings to his "Aztec Princess," promising a good future, promising happiness. The young man was both insanely possessive and insanely loving. We knew whatever the story was (had she thrown these hundreds of letters away because he was finally out of jail? Or because she had left him?) that it was a true and full story, the way lives are, and it filled us with wonder.

Perhaps, after all, this is the main reason we dive: for interesting views into interesting lives, for the stories that are being discarded before they can be shared.

There are certain guidelines to be followed while diving: Wear gloves and old clothing that covers, bring a small stepladder, look for moving vans, go at the end of months and especially at the end of semesters in our college town, go to the rich neighborhoods, but specifically, to the rich townhouses, where Dumpsters (instead of cans) are the norm. Never leave a mess. Bring a ski pole to use as a stick to bring things up or poke through bags. Tidy things up the way they were, or even better. Recycle what can be recycled. Winter is better than summer simply because of the smell. Leave anything with someone's identification (we don't want to be accused of being identity thieves). Understand that 90 percent of the world's population would love to have this stuff and that we live in a nation of self-centered, materialistic people. And mostly, try not to get depressed. So many beautiful things get thrown away.

My son, Jake, loves to leap out of the car and heave his little body into the Dumpsters. He's got my "finder gene," and he spends the majority of his time searching: for treasures, criminals, fossils, and gold nuggets in the river. So he loves diving, for the simple reason that he's bound to find something terrific every time. My daughter, who is four, prefers to sit inside the car and sift through whatever items come in. She lays claim to about three-fourths of them.

On a cloudy, blustery day, Jake and I are in the Dumpster. He's bright eyed and pink cheeked and busy handing things out to Tim. "Ellie will like this," he says, handing Tim a sequined pink bathrobe meant for someone who's five times her size.

What Jake's hoping for is another ten-gallon container of beer bottlecaps (some college student's proud collection, no doubt). Tim found one once, and Jake has been making things out of bottlecaps ever since—primarily knight armor and shields. Instead, he finds, to his great delight, a Twister game. He's set, his day has been made.

But there is more, and he's trying to hand out a cheap pastel print of a cat in a cracked-glass frame, and Tim keeps trying to explain the concept of "high-ending it," by which he means taking out only the good stuff. But Jake wants everything, and generally we relent, filling the car with stuff that we might re-Dumpster again.

"I hope we can do this next Saturday," Jake says, as he climbs out, and he says it again while he waits for Tim and me to retrieve the heavy adult-needed item: a perfectly good, large filing cabinet. Tim and I struggle with it, and I try to make sure I get most of the weight. But I see him wincing; something about the way we're walking is causing him pain somewhere.

I worry about Tim. Tomorrow he will probably, as he puts it, "have a bad day" as the result of today's fun. For days at a time, he disappears into his pain and comes out shaking like a dog from slumber and ready to dive again. When I know that his pain has increased, I stomp around wishing there was something I could do. I wish to zap his pain out into the universe, far away. I wish to have the land that he knows, and loves, offer some remedy. I wish for a miracle cure. I wish he would win the lottery.

When he is feeling good, and we walk, and talk, and he teaches me the geology of a region, or where to find a vein of calcite crystal, or shows my son clamshell fossils, then it is a joyous friendship. Simply, and wonderfully, a friendship. We swap funny stories, prowl around the river near his house, swap books, talk movies. And we rescue filing cabinets, and we dive.

Tim is forever pulling broken electrical items, such as fans, out of the Dumpster. I argue that we should leave them, but he insists on getting them so that we can tediously extract the copper from the motors. "Copper is a buck sixty a pound!" he says this in an animated, excited voice, but I'm no fool. By now, I've learned that we're going to spend an hour sitting around his picnic table, extracting a half a pound of copper: not a good day's wages, even for a writer. But he insists. Then we will go on "a metal run," where he sells the metal to the recycling center. We'll spend an afternoon loading all the stuff into the back of his rickety old flatbed trailer. Then we'll make the trek there, with my kids, who now know more about metals, and the prices they bring, than I ever will. (They also say things like, "Mom, you're the best mom, because if you suddenly die, we know how to live out of Dumpsters!")

On the way to the metal place, Tim talks: "Just stay with me here, this is important." (He says this because I'm tired and hot and smelly and want to go home.) "One ton of aluminum produced from bauxite consumes the energy equivalent of 356 barrels of oil (that's 197 million Btus). One pound of coal produced from an average strip mine in Wyoming can produce about 7,500 Btus. A pound of coal burned produces about 2.5 pounds of carbon dioxide, the primary greenhouse gas! Every can we pick out of a Dumpster basically saves a pound of carbon dioxide from being vented into the atmosphere!"

I spot a canister of sidewalk chalk on the floor of Tim's car—something he's no doubt recently retrieved from a Dumpster. The kids and I take it outside and draw pictures of the universe and the earth on the blacktop while the guys unload and weigh everything.

"Cool," says Jake. "Mom, can I have a turtle as a pet?"

"Mom, I have to pee," says Ellie.

I sigh. "No," I say to Jake. "You've got a lizard and rabbits and a dog and fish." To Ellie I say, "There's a bathroom at the metal place. Cross your legs if you have to."

The guys at the metal place wave as we drive in. They know us by now, and they like to chat with my kids. Tim backs up his car, which smells now of beer and stickiness, and when he stops, the men come forward, ready to unload all the metal we've brought today.

I spot a canister of sidewalk chalk on the floor of Tim's car—something he's no doubt recently retrieved from a Dumpster. The kids and I take it outside and draw pictures of the universe and the earth on the blacktop while the guys unload and weigh everything. Comets and planets and shooting stars appear everywhere—healthy and bright and beautiful.

Finally, the workers are done: we have 108 pounds of cans (that's about 3,215 of those babies), 400 pounds of extruded aluminum, 10 pounds of clean and dirty copper, 174 of radiators (aluminum/copper mixed), 116 pounds of insulated wire, 26 pounds of #1 single wire, 25 pounds of soft lead, 23 pounds of stainless steel, 30 pounds of yellow brass, and a bunch of batteries.

Assuming that the aluminum would be produced by a coal-fired power system, we have saved 18,000 pounds (nine tons) of carbon dioxide from being released into the air. That's 56 million Btus. Add to that the copper—about 175 pounds—which saves another 10 million Btus (and an additional 3,000 pounds of carbon dioxide from being emitted). And we're just talking about the aluminum and copper here; we're not even talking about how much earth would have been stripped, processed, and laid waste in a tailings pile left to further pollute. Plus, my son with his first hundred-dollar bill in his hand!

Before we load up and go home, Tim suggests we go diving next Sunday again. Everyone lets out a loud cheer, and so does a mountainside and the sky. At least I like to think so; that's the *real* treasure here. I glance at our picture of the universe on blacktop and wink. I tell you, it's enough to keep the heart happy.

PART TWO

Home Recycling

Gleaning from and for Our Homes

Just Imagine

RUTH FRIESEN

Ruth Friesen lives in Albuquerque, New Mexico, and has filled her home with treasures she bought at ReStore. After three years of working at ReStore and helping customers find inventive uses for gleaned objects, she is now channeling her creativity toward photography and writing. Ever the entrepreneur, she recently launched Silver Lining Moves, a service to assist seniors as they downsize their homes. This is her first published essay.

"What's this?" I pulled a piece of metal from the pile. It was rusty, but the shape intrigued me. Was it a bird cage? A store display? A giant eggbeater? No matter what it was, I knew I could use it to make something interesting.

I was standing in the backyard of a city-condemned house, and here was a lifetime of work of the retired welder who once had lived here. He missed his vocation so much that he spent his spare time welding literally tons of metal into fences, gazebos, and whatever else he could imagine. Once these items had been car wheels, window frames, I-beams holding up buildings, and now they were part of a welder's fantasy.

Once these items had been car wheels, window frames, I-beams holding up buildings, and now they were part of a welder's fantasy.

What I had come to see today, though, was a spiral staircase. The staircase was welded into other fanciful curlicues of metal, creating a fence, but it led nowhere—just upwards into the sky. Did the welder use it for stargazing if he had time after his day's welding? I recognized a kindred spirit in the welder. Maybe he didn't have a specific use for something, but he recognized its beauty, even though to the new owner it was five tons of metal to recycle.

This was one of many potential donations I previewed as the director of ReStore, a Habitat for Humanity building-material thrift store in Albuquerque. The very first treasure we gleaned even before the store opened was maple flooring. After nearly a year of searching for a suitable building for the store, I found a 1940s-era roller rink in an area with other thrift stores that fit my vision. Its maple floor was warped in places but still salvageable. So our volunteers set to work gently pulling up the floor and removing the nails. One of our first customers was overjoyed to find enough old-fashioned true-dimension maple flooring for his entire Craftsman-style home.

Opening the store had been a dream of mine ever since I read about a Habitat for Humanity thrift store in another city. Throughout the United States, hundreds of ReStores have sprung up. Habitat for Humanity discovered that selling donated, used building materials creates a revenue stream that enables the construction of more homes for low-income families.

"Why don't we have a ReStore?" I wondered. I approached the executive director of the Greater Albuquerque Habitat for Humanity, and, in response to my questions she said, "See what you can do." Ah, the challenge had been made. I mounted my white horse (really a white Infiniti) and rode off to conquer.

Finding the initial inventory for the store was not a problem. For years, folks had been calling Habitat for Humanity wanting to donate a door, some windows, the sink they had just pulled from their bathroom, appliances, and all kinds of items they thought we might use in building homes for low-income families. And for years, they had been turned away because the policy of Habitat is to use only new construction material and to build to a standardized plan with few modifications, making building simple for volunteers. But for a while, the Habitat staff had been saying "Yes" to these donors, and now there was a warehouse of goods to be sorted through and sold. I counted thirty-five ceiling fans, a myriad of doors, windows, stoves, and sinks, and even a pale pink bathroom stall. Amid these treasures were three thousand partially used cans of paint, which the warehouse neighbors were delighted to receive.

I'm not above Dumpster diving for items to sell. I've retrieved a bunk bed from the Dumpster behind a furniture rental store and books and brass candlesticks from a flea market. In my neighborhood, I once found five professionally handcrafted platters in a bin on the curb. When I pass home remodeling sites, I always want to stop and rummage through the Dumpster for reusable material. With nearly a million people, there is no shortage of Dumpsters in Albuquerque.

Nationwide, the amount of construction waste is staggering. In 2003, the EPA estimated that 164,000 tons of building-related waste was generated, 38 percent of which was renovation waste. I have left notes on windows leaning against the big roll-off bins in driveways, asking homeowners and contractors to consider donating reusable items rather than heaving them. They usually donate and then spread the word about ReStore to their friends.

Used material is treasure to landlords, our best customers. Unwilling to put a lot of money into something that often gets wrecked by tenants, they find gently and not-so-gently used cabinets, better light fixtures, and other items. When we receive a donation of apartment-size stoves from a landlord redoing a large complex, the stoves are gone within hours to other landlords. Small-job contractors and handymen working with homeowners on repairs and remodels love our store too. One homeowner bought the welder's spiral staircase to access the deck he was creating atop his flat-roof garage. Another struggled home with a whole wall of windows removed from some palatial house.

The most commonly donated items—windows, doors, and appliances—are also the most in demand. Often, new homeowners plan to use them simply as they were intended to be used, but sometimes they see opportunities to create something unique with ordinary materials. One flower lover used hollow-core doors for shelves and sliding-glass patio doors to form a small greenhouse just outside her kitchen window. An artist's group took advantage of a one-dollar door sale to buy fifty doors to use as canvas stretchers. Hung horizontally, a peeling yellow-painted French door sans glass helps define my office space, and a louvered closet door hides a support post.

Full sets of kitchen cabinets sell immediately, even if they are 30-plus years old. When the store first opened, we received a batch of baby-pink cabinets. Judging from the details, such as rounded corners on the backs of the drawers, they were from the 1940s. We even got the pink dishwasher. Being new at this and wanting to get this pile moved out, I priced the whole set at one hundred dollars. It sold in a week. I soon learned that our customers had the vision needed to modify and update to make things work. Pink is no problem as long as you have paint.

Using cabinets, one customer created a captain's bed. She found enough drawer units of similar size and height to serve as the foundation and storage drawers under a mattress platform. A low metal cabinet with wheels inspired another to create an ottoman by adding a foam rubber top. Built-in oven cabinets are often orphans awaiting just the right size oven, which doesn't happen very often. I urge customers to fill the vacant oven space with shelves, and, voila, a space-saving storage cabinet for a hobby room is born. One day when the stars shone upon us just right, I helped a customer sort through our pile of orphan drawers and found enough of the right size to fit the oven space. Orphans no more.

Once, a discouraged customer approached the cash register empty-handed after looking for something in which to display her jewelry at a craft show. Scouting the drawers aisle again yielded a large, shallow drawer just the right size. The next aisle produced piano hinges and Plexiglas. Rummaging in miscellaneous parts, we discovered round, wooden knobs for feet, and a display case was created. Another artist found that pegboard created perfect ventilated sides for a carrying case for her oil paintings.

I kept waiting for an artist to see the wealth of possibilities in several oak wine barrels, dismantled stave by stave, which were donated by a vineyard. I envisioned painted vignettes hung as a mobile, scalloped crown molding around a dining nook cove, rocking chair feet, garden edging, candleholders, or street and name signs. During a visit to a bed-and-breakfast in Oregon wine country, I saw a rocking chair made from barrel staves. But, alas, no artist with such a vision appeared in Albuquerque. Sadly, we gave them away as kindling.

What might be viewed as kindling by one person may inspire creativity in another. When a plumbing supply company donated parts bins that had been sitting outside for many months, we wondered if we could salvage anything from them. Teenage volunteers painted some of the bins a shiny turquoise for our electrical parts aisle. They now hold switchplates, plugs, and cords. We also use them when giving directions. "See those turquoise bins? Go to the aisle just past them." Unpainted bins form a dividing wall between our workshop area and the sold-merchandise area. A restaurateur, one of our steady customers, begged and pleaded with us to sell him one for a wine rack for his new Brazilian churrasco. We finally relented and watched him drive away with one end hanging perilously off the end of his pickup truck.

After a Whole Foods store renovation, I wondered what our creative customers would find to do with the large, wooden produce tables and bins that were donated. The bins were snapped up in a springtime rush of planting fervor as large flowerbeds. With their pullout shelves, the tables became ideal hobbyists' tables. Another renovation yielded fourteen-inch copper letters. They became decorative accents in a home stager's repertoire and in many people's homes. When people ask me why I have a "Y" in my kitchen, I answer, "Why not?" And a copper "Pastries" sign hangs as a room divider near my kitchen.

Not all of the imagination goes into turning discards into décor. Sometimes the practical uses are just as imaginative. A boot-clad young cowpoke ambled in one day from his ranch a hundred miles away looking for solutions to a very muddy yard. When we told him he could take away our excess pallets to make a walkway, a wide grin lit up his face under his broad, black hat.

Ordinary bathtubs are a dime a dozen, or nearly. Sometimes we can't even give them away. But to a dog lover, they are the remedy for muddy paw prints—a dog bath situated near the back door. They even could use the gray water stored in the tub by another customer.

Even the most mundane material can be reused imaginatively. Eyeing a section of metal ductwork languishing on our shelves for over a year, I envisioned a planter. "Yeah, right, you see a planter in everything," my employees scoffed. But when I opened a furniture annex to ReStore, I finally had the opportunity to use that ductwork, four sections joined together with an opening at the top of each section. Drilling holes for a couple of chains enabled me to hang it from the ceiling in front of the store windows and fill it with plants. If customer comments are any indication, this summer Albuquerque will have many patios with similar hanging planters. And we sold out of ductwork.

Envisioning how furniture can be reused is the ultimate high for me. That wobbly pine table still would work in a potting shed. An ornately carved headboard could be mounted above a mantel or grace the landing of a staircase. Instead of holding a canopy, spiraled bedposts create a furniture look under a kitchen counter or finish off a countertop to the beamed ceiling. In my house, wooden lampstands become candleholders and display seashells. If I could find another low cabinet, I'd use portions of wooden lamps for ottoman legs. But sometimes a lamp is just a lamp. One customer, a movie property manager, asked me, "What period do you think this furniture is?" When my reply was "1970s," she agreed and took three knobby gold-glassed lamps, two chairs, and a blue flower-print couch. One day soon, someone will be sitting in a theater watching a movie and exclaim, "I used to have a couch just like that."

Perhaps the most imaginative customers are the crafters. I wouldn't have thought of wrapping wire and beads around flat glass panels from outdated chandeliers to make suncatchers. And who would have thought of weaving coils of nail-gun nails through rabbit fencing to make a decorative fence? In their skilled hands, glass globes become bird feeders and planters. Knobby, clear lamp bases hold candles or become terrariums, and broken tile is patterned into tabletops and stove backsplashes.

Recycling does have its limits. Who wants a large hot tub with holes punched in the acrylic? And how do we dispose of it when it is dumped on our doorstep? Do cheap, outdated fiberboard cabinets ever become sought-after antiques? But then again, who would have thought that metal kitchen cabinets would become highly desired additions to a retro kitchen? Many people would have thought the old sink filled with paint was useless. But it was just the ticket for a rough-and-tumble hermit who was building a cabin in the mountains for less than five thousand dollars. The fact that it had no holes for faucets was perfect for his pump sitting next to the sink.

I've learned to view each item as something intriguing, an opportunity for a second use that may be even better than its first use. As my guests walk up my curved, pebbled sidewalk, past the cactus and to my front door, they often ask me if that oval wiry globe on a rusted metal porch spindle is a birdcage. It could be, I suppose. It began its life as a commercial dough mixer, and then it was that welder's treasure. For me, it's the perfect sculpture in a spot where only cactus grows. I think the welder would be proud.

Wood Blues

PAUL MILLER

Paul Miller was raised near Lake Erie; then he found a second place of power a few decades ago close to the heart of the Rockies. He was named Artist-in-Residence for 2007 in Rocky Mountain National Park, and his creative nonfiction has appeared in *Pulse of the River, The Sand Papers,* and *High Country News.* "Wood Blues" is a story of the near-death and ultimate rescue of blue-stain pine, with supporting roles played by bugs and the warp of geologic time.

I first became enamored of blue-stain wood—a creation of pine beetles—the moment I stepped into a vacant house for sale in a town along the northern reaches of the Front Range of Colorado. I was with Annie, who a year later would become my wife, and we'd decided that the apartment where we lived was becoming too claustrophobic. We needed a house to make into a home, a place to stretch out our lives a bit.

We pulled up in front of a one-story clapboard house in the middle of the block. This place, built in 1929, felt different right away, with its centered door, wide front porch open to the world, generous eaves, and low-angled roofline. The front room of the small house especially captivated us. Expansive windows faced all sides of the compass except east, and light flooded the room. The walls needed paint, and the carpet was marginal, but the prize, for me, was the east wall of the front room, which stood out like a shrine: blue-stain pine paneling ranged from ceiling to floor, and I couldn't take my eyes off it. The lodgepole pine, cut a true three-quarters of an inch thick, was a deep, golden hue, with streaks of gray, tan, and blue running through the wood. The panels weren't perfect—a few of the tongue-and-groove joints didn't quite match, and the wood was nicked and cracked in places from years of aging in the dry climate—but still the blue-stain made the bare room inviting.

Standing in the living room, I drifted into a waking dream, knowing with more certainty that this would be our new home. How could we lose, coming home to such warmth? The wood panels alone were the perfect embodiment of the way nature shows off its artistry. But when Annie started talking about how blue stain forms in the wood—she's a botanist, and takes care of the science while I indulge in esoterica—I moved from daydreaming to hearing the nuts and bolts about the process. The fungus that colors the wood, as I found out, is usually spread by bark beetles. Though some purists think stain ruins the wood (one preventative measure calls for dousing green lumber in tetrachlorophenol before shipping), I couldn't stop looking at this lovely palette and seeing stories behind the complex hues, the life cycle of a pine coming to a close in some valley, a beetle carrying spores (*Ceratocystis*, Annie said) into the wood and leaving a gallery of colors behind. I imagined the tree crashing to the ground in a windstorm, then draft horses pulling the log out of the forest. Sawyers with shavings in their beards would shape the wood into raw boards, then send the rough planks to other markets to produce the finished wall panels. Such a bucolic scene, so far removed from the vast tracts of clear-cuts that dot the planet like scabs.

I couldn't stop looking at this lovely palette and seeing stories behind the complex hues, the life cycle of a pine coming to a close in some valley, a beetle carrying spores (Ceratocystis, Annie said) into the wood and leaving a gallery of colors behind. I imagined the tree crashing to the ground in a windstorm, then draft horses pulling the log out of the forest.

On this February day, though, logging wasn't my primary concern. Within ten seconds of stepping into the house, we were imagining the rooms full of our books and chairs and artwork and friends. Such an easy choice for us both: we'd never had trouble making big decisions from the moment we met in the frozen backcountry of Yellowstone several years earlier, not with finances, not with traveling together for months overseas, not with buying a house together. We'd decide to do something life-altering; then we'd go barreling out and do it.

Weeks later, we signed the dense, scary contract, and became homeowners for the first time.

Over the next fifteen years, we filled the house with dust from renovations. Meanwhile, I ramped up my love affair with woodworking, hanging my tools on straight, solid walls and laying out cabinet frames on the level floor of the garage.

I also continued struggling with the process of how the wood turned up in my hands to begin with. Over the years, I'd seen the effects of what logging has done to the landscape, and I could no longer pretend the damage didn't matter. Walking down the aisle at a local warehouse, I'd see the logo of a lumber company stamped on a huge bundle of redwood or Douglas fir, and feel my face redden. How much old growth was sacrificed for this wood? How many species were displaced when a forest slope was clear-cut? How many tons of sediments were choking streams from unchecked runoff?

And, face red, I'd pick up a few planks of wood anyway, because it wasn't much and because I had a project to do. I figured that even the blue-stain pine on the wall of my house probably was logged in mountain valleys west of my home, and I wasn't about to atone for that sin.

I did manage to assuage my guilt by living more carefully. If I had to contribute to the felling of trees, then at least I could reduce my footprint on the planet elsewhere. I believed—still do, fervently—that owning lots of stuff and maximizing convenience can be as damaging as unchecked harvesting of natural resources.

Not that long ago, life was much leaner, and "conservation" wasn't such a catchphrase. During a construction project on our home, we opened up an outside wall and discovered that the small back room had been added some years after the house had first been built. To help insulate the wall, the ends of the siding had been stuffed with pieces of cloth. Excavating further, we found more insulation: remnants of cardboard and newspaper tacked inside the wall. One small piece of newspaper pasted to stiff paperboard featured a cartoon from 1924 called "Harold Teen—The Sage and the Sheik."

The paper was being used as insulation. I loved the idea. As much as I considered myself a devout reuser, this old newspaper, as brown and fragile as ancient parchment, easily beat my best efforts. Like a time capsule, the newspaper spoke of an era long gone, when people used what they had and used it well until nothing was left. Careful conservation of resources has largely been lost to us, and we're poorer for it.

Standing in the shell of what would be a new room, I thought about how different our requirements were now, the two of us frenzied about adding a room in spite of our efforts to simplify.

"You know," Annie said to me later, reading my mood, "we're really not going overboard with our needs. We're making our home better so the next family won't have to worry about things like furnaces and pipes and where to put a new baby."

How could I argue? Just the garage alone, the one we spent one summer building, would last a hundred years. The only thing I missed about the old garage, in fact, was the faint but distinct smell of hay after a rainstorm, a deeply pleasing scent that told me there once may have been horses on our property. Catching that scent on a damp afternoon always made me want to saddle up a horse and go looking for a choice piece of downed wood to drag home.

"Yeah, and nobody will have to go crazy laying down fifty feet of extension cord to plug in a lamp," I said. "Besides, cardboard and newspaper probably don't have very high insulating values." Our new addition had enough fiberglass insulation to keep us warm at temperatures cold enough to crack open trees.

But then, being true (and paradoxical) Americans in a land of excess, and because we seemed to be bumping into each other more and more, we eventually agreed we were out of room. Not all at once, but slowly, reluctantly, we finally decided to leave our home of fifteen years.

We told ourselves that it was okay to expand our living space because we wouldn't be building a new home. Instead of chewing up resources constructing a place from the foundation up, we'd just look for what I cheerfully called a "used home." Kind of the ultimate in recycling, I told Annie, but she knew that anyway. What better way to use resources than to move into a place someone else had abandoned and fill it with our lives?

It would be hard to move, hard especially to leave the beautiful, blue-stain pine in the living room, upon which hung landscape photos, family portraits, and a long, narrow Chinese scroll that Annie had bought from a village artist along the Yangtze River, with its ethereal drawing of chrysanthemums and a bluebird perched on a bamboo limb. I'd never touched that pine paneling, except to tap in hangers. It never needed to be touched. Whenever I opened the front door after being gone for weeks, the intricately veined pine was the first thing I saw. It was a gift, like coming home to warm flames in a fireplace.

We found a used home on the south side of town, a roomy place built in 1988 with light pouring into the rooms and easy access to bike trails and local stores. This would be the last, biggest, greatest place we would ever need, we told each other, clinking wine glasses in a toast before unpacking boxes.

After most of our home was settled, I set up my woodworking equipment in the spacious garage and, accompanied by chattering house finches in the blue spruces lining the driveway, began building furniture for our new place.

I've come to accept that, no matter what I do, I'll leave a footprint on the landscape. Every home I've lived in was built of wood, but all that material, gathered from live, growing trees, was put to good use providing shelter and warmth for generations of families. Where once I would cringe whenever I loaded rough-milled lumber into the back of my truck, I now vow to make the best possible use of the wood, to craft it carefully into something aesthetic and useful and solid enough to last a long time.

After finishing a cherry table lamp for a wedding present to a niece, or an oak and maple table for our own home, I'd squirrel

away all the scrap—ridiculously small pieces—in bins and on
shelves in the garage. At times, I'd try getting rid of some of the
scrap. I'd set an empty trash can in the middle of the garage and
steel myself to heave away. But it never worked. I'd end up throwing
away only warped pieces of beat-up plywood. Closely inspecting a
two-inch-square piece of curly maple, holding it over the maw of
the trash can, I'd get lost imagining how many ways it could still
be of use. Maybe it could be part of a child's toy, a pull for a fence
gate, or a drawer stop for a dresser. The scrap then would become
magical, a living thing full of potential, and so it would rejoin the
other small pieces in a dusty storage cabinet.

I've also accepted that we humans aren't the only species to
take what's needed from the land, leaving behind profound and
sometimes irreversible changes. Vast stands of pine, some of which
become stained with the array of color I'm so enamored of, are now
being obliterated by the same tiny creatures that helped create the
effect. Armies of bark beetles, western pine beetles, roundheaded
pine beetles, mountain pine beetles—a few of the six thousand or
so species in the weevil family—chew into the cambium layer of
trees to set up their homes, to reproduce, to move on to other
conifers. Left are ravaged neighborhoods of dead and dying trees.

Even healthy trees are no match for heavy infestations of beetles,
something that's happening in places overseas as well as right here
in the Rocky Mountains. In some areas, trees with no commercial
value that are being destroyed may still have value to other life,
but the bugs don't care. In and around Yellowstone, the mountain
pine beetle (*Dendroctonus ponderosae*—what a lyrical name for a
killer) is exterminating vast tracts of whitebark pines, the seeds of
which are a major, seasonal food source for Clark's nutcrackers,
red squirrels, and grizzlies. And with recent average increases in
global temperatures, the beetles are feasting in places that once were
too cold to support them.

So, being human and needing to fuss over our planet, we argue
about what to do. Let forests die, since it's part of the natural order?
Cut ahead of infestations to create buffer zones? Set fires? Use

noxious chemicals? Pray for long, frigid winters? I see this struggle between our own prolific human species and the voracious species of bugs, and I think: what's better, who's more deserving? A chainsaw and lumberyard, or beetles and square miles of tasty trees? Who needs the wood more? Who will be here in ten thousand years to create beautiful blue-stain works of art?

I often think back to a moment I experienced some years before in the kitchen of our old home. I was gazing out the window, watching the wind blowing leaves into tiny whirlwinds in the narrow side yard. The sun was low in the west, and I could see dust and insects swirling around with the leaves, dancing in the late autumn heat. I became more and more entranced until, for an exquisite moment, I could see the house next door fall to pieces, the landscape absorbing all its contents over the course of thousands of years until nothing was left but prairie grasses and shrubs and remnants of cotton-wood leaves swirling in the wind. The world to the horizon was green and thriving, without a building in sight. At that moment, I felt to my core that nothing we humans did, nothing we built, would change the inexorable forces of decay and dust and rebirth that happen on unimaginable scales. Nothing within our grasp would make us see any clearer how geologic time reduces our best efforts to an infinitesimal shrug. My own shell, the carapace that allowed me to move around in self-made worlds, was for that instant mean-ingless. I had been absorbed into the earth as easily as water playing on a forest floor.

For four months we owned two homes, but then we found good people—acquaintances—who were anxious to buy our old place.

"Nichole and I know how much you guys took care of your house," Arthur told us over and over. "We'd love the chance to continue taking good care of the place, just like you did."

So we made a deal and wished them all the best. I had visions of them settling comfortably into the odd-shaped rooms and wandering around for days, for weeks, admiring our handiwork, bragging about how the former owners had left them with almost nothing to do, and how nice it was to just sink into a place and unpack boxes.

I carried that notion with me when I stopped by to pick up some mail, two days after Nichole and Arthur moved into the house. From the sidewalk, I could hear hammering and loud voices and music coming from inside. Something was going on that didn't seem right to me. I fought the urge to flee.

I knocked on the front door. Through the screen, I could see a pile of lumber stacked haphazardly in the living room. Before fully realizing it, I knew what I was looking at.

Arthur came to the door, threw it open with his usual bonhomie, and invited me in. I stood transfixed. Mere hours after getting the house keys from us, he had torn off every last blue-stain pine board and had tossed them all into an ignominious pile, a heap of pickup sticks. Finishing nails stuck out of the wood like broken teeth.

I may have smiled, I don't know. It was hard to not smile around Arthur, with his goofy grin and good nature. Instead of fainting (I was close), I asked with dry mouth what he intended to do with the wood.

"Dunno," he said, anxious to show me what else he'd been doing to the rest of our house. His house now, an impossible concept. "Probably haul it to the landfill. Want some of it?"

I stood paralyzed in what had once been my place of power and stared at the naked wall, the indecently exposed wall, an ugly scar of decrepit plaster and lath. Arthur rattled on and on about how cool the living room would look after he was done, but I couldn't absorb any of it. Had I missed something all these years? Had other people visited and seen the tongue-and-groove as cheap and annoying, as some kitsch remnant from a bygone era? Could such warm wood have failed to touch the heart of this man, this young couple, as well-meaning as they were?

Ridiculous questions, but in the throes of trauma, I was grasping for anything to distract me. This was not my home anymore, and Arthur could rip the ceiling open to the sky if he wanted. At least I could salvage what he felt was useless. The landfill, sweet God in heaven.

"I'll be glad to take it off your hands," I finally managed. "Good thing I drove my truck over."

I spent a half hour loading all the paneling into the bed of my truck, then scavenged around the living room looking for scraps, for any small slivers of wood. I felt like a forensic expert combing the scene of a crime.

A short time later I said good-bye, then drove slowly back to my new home, the wood behind me rattling like bones dancing a jig.

One wall of our basement is now covered in tongue-and-groove blue-stain pine, originally milled to an honest three-quarters of an inch thick.

Every cut I make in the wood—there's still some left—releases the haunting scent of antiquity, the countless years of trees standing against blistering winter winds. Particles of sun and rain, inscribed deeply in the grain, cover my arms in a dusting of light gold powder. Blue and gray veins, memorials of *Ceratocystis* spores, trace a meandering river of color, a map laid out in living fiber in a forest long since gone. Not a single one of us will ever know where that neighborhood once stood.

Throwing Out the
Dishwater

SUSAN J. TWEIT

A plant ecologist who once studied sagebrush and grizzly bear habitat, Susan J. Tweit believes that humans belong to what Aldo Leopold called "the community of the land." Her concern about the impact of even the most mundane of daily activities led her to begin throwing out the dishwater, and then writing about it. She is the author of ten books as well as articles and commentaries featured in media as diverse as *Audubon,* the *Los Angeles Times, High Country News, Popular Mechanics,* and *Martha Stewart Living Radio.* She also saves trees by publishing her work online at susanjtweit.com.

Once I lived in a one-room log cabin where I pumped my water from a well and heated it on a woodstove. When I was finished washing my dishes, I carried the dishpan outside and tossed the water on the nearby sagebrush.

It seemed natural to me to return the water to the same ground I pumped it from. The extra "rain" from my dishpan nurtured the patch of sagebrush off my tiny porch, keeping it green and fragrant even in dry years. I was careful not to foul my supply: my disposal

Once I lived in a one-room log cabin where I pumped my water from a well and heated it on a woodstove.

site was far from the well itself, and the groundwater deep beneath the surface was buffered by the natural filter of soil atop layers of porous gravel.

Nowadays my house is serviced via pipes from the main under the street. Water appears at the twist of a faucet handle and vanishes in a swirl down the drain, with no effort on my part. Such easy access is a mixed blessing. My valley, along with other areas of the West, is entering its tenth year of drought, despite recent snows. After watching an extraordinary February heat wave suck the snow off the peaks and the moisture from the soil, I grew more and more uneasy.

Water is a limited commodity here, but you wouldn't know it by turning on your tap. No matter the amount of precipitation we receive—whether briefly generous or so scant it portends drought— our municipal supply pours out unchecked. (Our rural town installed water meters less than a decade ago, and only because state law required metering. There are still those here who view the meters as part of an ongoing conspiracy designed to divert more water to wealthy urban Colorado for its acres of lawns, and a threat to rural life, liberty, and the pursuit of impoverished self-determination.)

I miss the effort I used to expend on drawing water: turn on the pump, wait for it to pull liquid from below the surface, open the faucet to fill the storage vessels, and lug them down the hill and across the porch into the cabin.

The pumping time and flow varied from season to season and year to year with the variation in precipitation. Carrying the water from pump to cabin gave me direct feedback on my consumption: at seven pounds per gallon, I felt every cup. It was a powerful incentive for conservation.

I'm not going to rip out my plumbing. Still, when late winter turned in hot and dry, I wanted to do something to honor the reality of the water supply I depend on. After some discussion, my husband and I bought a dishpan to collect the water from our kitchen sink, which we pour onto our compost pile.

The dishpan holds 11.4 quarts, slightly less than 3 gallons, and we empty it three times a day. That's a little over 8 gallons of water, a small fraction of the 271 gallons each person in my community consumes per day on average. But it's enough to remind me that the water I use does not come free: energy to run pumps and purifiers and to add manufactured chemicals is required to move it from ditches and wells to my house to sewage plant to river.

Spilling the dishwater onto my compost pile, I am returning some of what I use every day to the soil, where it can percolate through the layers, cleansed by the lives under the surface, and recharge the aquifer I draw from.

I'm also breaking the law. Colorado water law allows consumers just one use, not two, before returning the water to the nearest river. The Uniform Plumbing Code defines dishwater as "blackwater," the equivalent of household toxic waste, and forbids its disposal except into septic or sewage systems.

The first infraction is a technicality, the second a matter of sanitation. Ours is vegetarian dishwater, free of the animal flesh and fat that cause contamination, so I am confident of the ability of the microbes in our compost pile to sanitize it at least as well as any sewage plant.

Throwing out our dishwater won't solve my community's water problems, but it will hone my awareness. It is a private act, an everyday ritual that links me to the consequences of my actions: the more water I use, the more dishpans I haul.

It is also a spiritual choice. By taking responsibility for my used water instead of consigning it to someone else down the drain, I commit myself to honesty about my impact on this landscape. In that small way, I acknowledge that my fate rests with that of the community of beings dependent on the natural cycles of weather and water and time.

As I spill out the dishwater, I honor the connection between the water that sustains my life and the piece of earth I call home.

Home Recycling

JEFFE KENNEDY

Jeffe Kennedy took the crooked road to writing, stopping off at neurobiology, religious studies, and environmental consulting before her creative writing began appearing in places like *Redbook, Mountain Living, Wyoming Wildlife,* and *Under the Sun.* She has been a Ucross Foundation Fellow and received first place from Pronghorn Press for its *Dry Ground* anthology. She is also a Wyoming Arts Council roster artist and recipient of the council's 2005 Doubleday Award and 2007 Fellowship for Poetry. Jeffe has contributed to several anthologies—*Drive: Women's True Stories of the Open Road, Hard Ground,* and *Bombshells.* Her first collection, *Wyoming Trucks, True Love, and the Weather Channel,* was published by University of New Mexico Press in 2004. Jeffe lives in an old house in Laramie, Wyoming, with two Maine coon cats, a border collie, and a fish pathologist, all lightly used, in excellent condition.

The letter to the editor complained bitterly about the city council's foolish and shortsighted decision against a new housing development. The author, new to our town, listed among his righteous points the dearth of available housing to buy, particularly since he was too smart to consider "investing in a pre–World War II house."

As one delighted with the council's wise and far-reaching judgment, I wondered at those who disdain old houses. The house David and I share is not only pre–WWII, like so many of the houses that form the core of our small Wyoming town, but—to the letter writer's great dismay—it's pre–WWI and, rather than an albatross, our prize.

Perhaps we are foolish. Neither of us has ever been the type to embrace the latest thing. Only when cassette tapes vanished from the stores did we make the concession to a CD player. Only when the newest movies were only on DVD did we abandon our videotape player for a dual model, so we could play both. We have computers to work on that have no joysticks or enhanced graphics cards and cell phones that play no songs, take no pictures. We've never owned a brand-new car.

I understand, to some extent, the desire for the brand-new thing. The fantasy that somehow it will last longer, that it will not break, will need no service calls. Perhaps it might quietly function with no maintenance for years.

The universe, we learned in physics, tends toward entropy. Everything breaks; everything falls apart into its components, and those components into their materials. Animal corpses and junkyard cars alike dissolve into dirt eventually. Entropy occurs all on its own, with no assistance from anyone. But to create something requires energy. One must invest energy into matter to create a thing.

The worst part is, once you labor to create the thing, you must labor to keep it. The moment you turn your back in satisfaction, entropy steps up admiringly and begins to take it apart again. I've long hated this about the world—that I can't invest just once. That I can't buy a black skirt of a certain style and then never buy it again. But inevitably after fifteen years, the skirt has worn out— my friends will point it out and shake their heads in affection for my foibles—and I'm forced to reacquire that same thing. I dig up the sod in my yard to create a flowerbed and forever after fight the grass blades that encroach, trying to unmake my garden and re-create their kingdom of lawn. For all I know, the grass thinks it's fighting entropy, too, when we simply struggle with each other to make the world how we most like it. I have intelligence and tools on my side, while grass blades persist through overwhelming numbers and singularity of purpose.

Perhaps if I engaged in a single purpose I would feel less as if I run from project to project, not only creating new things, but shoring up the crumbling structures of the ones I've created in years past. So I understand why someone would not want an old house, why they'd like to hermetically seal themselves away from entropy in fresh drywall and the latest wiring technology.

I know I can't win the war against entropy, pit myself against the overwhelming force of the universe, but in my daily life I can win the little battles. In many ways, this is the meaning of life to me, to pit my skills into creating what the universe cannot immediately disassemble. But as much as I cheer on creation of any kind, I cannot condone creating what we already have. With less energy than creating a whole new thing, we can re-create in small ways and preserve against the pick, pick, picking of entropy.

So I find myself horrified at the proliferation of new houses. Like grass blades determined to create a uniform lawn, the housing developments seem to reproduce themselves along the Front Range, filling every fertile field with drywall and wiring and concrete driveways with a singularity of purpose beyond me. People need places to live, yet how could there possibly be the need for so many more places to live? For each farm replaced with a subdivision of myriad identical houses, I picture that same number of existing houses left empty somewhere else.

The world's population may be increasing by over seventy-seven million each year, but the U.S. population is only increasing by just over two million, counting both births and immigration. In 2006, 1.12 million new houses were sold, so at face value that sounds like it's meeting the population increase. Until you do some math and find that less than 69 percent of people actually own homes, and that 2.3 to 3.13 people live in each house. That makes nearly half a million more houses built each year than there are people to live in them. It makes me wonder what happens to the not-new houses. I imagine half a million old homes abandoned and left to rot in compromised neighborhoods, condemned to make way for office buildings and vacant lots alike. Arguments about limiting births and immigration aside, I find myself wondering if houses now are yet something else we metaphorically haul off to the landfill.

Yes, old houses can be more work. Our pre–WWI house sometimes creakingly conflicts with the modern era, requiring new pipes, some plaster patches. We were forced to rework the wiring to the garage after discovering that some long-past innovator buried an extension cord to do the job. Sure, it takes some energy, some re-creating. Sure, it takes some money. But then money is just another kind of energy—I put my energy into my job, for which they give me money so I can pay to maintain my shelter.

Our house also possesses charms far too expensive to build into today's new constructions. We may scorn our ancestors' wisdom in favor of new technology, but it's worth noting that the oldest parts of New Orleans survived Hurricane Katrina and the levee breaks. Blessed were those with homes in the old neighborhoods. And blessed we are with superior craftsmanship that seals out the winter winds that creep through the drywall and insulation gaps in the prefabs.

Yes, our house has been updated over the last one hundred years; a southern addition with double-paned glass and skylights contributes passive solar heating most welcome in our cold but sunny winters. Insulation has been crammed into nooks not designed for them. The furnace no longer burns coal, but runs efficiently on a computer-controlled thermostat. The house has been re-created with care. And though new building codes may render new houses more energy efficient per square foot, our old-fashioned modest square footage tips the scale back in our favor.

Also, a recent report shows that homes built before April 2006 will likely fail energy efficiency checks because of new insulation standards. That would certainly redefine "old" and "new" houses.

Yes, old houses can be more work. Our pre–WWI house sometimes creakingly conflicts with the modern era, requiring new pipes, some plaster patches. We were forced to rework the wiring to the garage after discovering that some long-past innovator buried an extension cord to do the job.

Like a Shakespearean hero, the seeds of America's downfall may indeed lie in what first made us great. The United States has long excelled, the wide world over, in innovation, in creating the newest, best, and latest. That has truly been our greatness, why our new country surged forward to lead the world in technology. Now we lead the world in consumption of energy resources and production of carbon dioxide. We may yet build ourselves into an early death.

In *An Inconvenient Truth*, Al Gore suggests that if we would just pause briefly between denial of what is happening to our world and despair that nothing can be done to change it, then we might find a small place to take action, to find an opportunity to make small changes in our lives. Change our thinking, he suggests.

There's an old saying that a European thinks one hundred miles is a long way and an American thinks one hundred years is a long time. Many of us come from Europeans, and other much older cultures, yet we understand that one hundred miles is but a small piece of our enormous land. Perhaps we can begin to understand that a house one hundred years old can be worthwhile? In their small lands, Europeans have been forced into using what is already in place. They renovate, rewire, and replumb houses that are five hundred years old, but they count the cost of filling their farms with subdivisions too high to do otherwise. In the insatiable desire for new houses, Americans show they count the cost of maintaining and re-creating old houses higher than sacrificing farmland.

When I see the cancer of new houses filling the Front Range, I do despair. And I know I can't fight it; none of us can, really. As long as people want new houses, new houses will be built. But perhaps we can change our thinking and not *want* the new houses. We can find the beauty in old houses. Recycle what already exists, re-create it, make it shine again. All of those new houses will become old ones in time. What will we do with them then?

PART THREE

Teach Me

Gleaning for and from People

What I Have Gleaned

TIM VAUGHAN

As a geologist, Tim Vaughan prospected all over the West before becoming a Dumpster diver and teacher of English as a second language. As this essay indicates, these two activities have become connected in interesting ways and highlight the deep schism between middle-class accoutrements left in the trash and his evenings with immigrants. This is his first published work.

There are twelve of them: Cosmin, Yen, Rati, Zulma, Victor, Leticia, Dolores, Thomas, Bing, Luciana, Terizina, and Lucy. Twice a week, they come in the evening to learn English from me. They are from six different countries.

Rati is from India and always shows up for class early, waits by the classroom door until I arrive, and then asks for permission to enter the room. She is thin, with long black hair, brown skin, and a bindi spot on her forehead. Looking at Rati reminds me of desert wash on the canyons walls of Utah—mixtures of browns, dark browns, and blacks. She will learn English fast, because she fearlessly and freely speaks broken English, and she is aggressive. She asks direct

Looking at Rati reminds me of desert wash on the canyons walls of Utah—mixtures of browns, dark browns, and blacks.

and specific questions, and although her native language is Tamil, she knows English grammar better than I do. Rati is desperately lonely. She arrived in the United States just a few months ago. She did not ask or want to come to America, but her parents found a good prospective husband who was attending college in America, the arrangement was agreed to by all parties, and now Rati waits for me every Monday and Wednesday evening. We are currently practicing giving and receiving directions in English. She tells me that she comes from a culture where everyone lives on top of each other and knows everyone else in the neighborhood. In addition, the streets are a tangle, so giving American-style directions would be impossible, impersonal, and rude. In my town, recently voted by *Money* magazine as a "Best Place to Live," she knows no one, except her husband and a few other Indians. She tells me that she tries to practice asking directions with the citizens of my fine town; she is shocked at the coldness of the upscale Anglos here. No one seems to have time to make a new friend, or even have the courtesy to pass the time.

Cosmin is from Romania and always wears a flannel shirt and jeans, which means that I automatically like him, because that's what I tend to wear. He habitually arrives at class very late and physically exhausted. Cosmin won the lottery, literally. Romania, like many countries, has a lottery to determine who wins the opportunity to get a work visa to the United States. I think the odds of winning this lottery are similar to the odds of winning a monetary lottery in the United States, but he was lucky, and so Cosmin and his wife arrived in the United States over a year ago. They tried Florida because of the large Romanian population there, and they enjoyed being around their fellow countrymen, but Cosmin missed the mountains of Romania. He missed camping. He missed nature. He says that in Romania you may be poor, but you can camp anywhere. So they moved to Vermont, but it was expensive, and he couldn't find anywhere to camp. People kept chasing him off their land. He didn't know any better. So they got out the map and looked again and found that Colorado had mountains. Cosmin found a job on a drywall crew. He cannot understand why when he hired on, his bosses did not tell him about the deductions that come out of his paycheck and lower his take-home pay, even though he uses some of these benefits. Cosmin does not like being fooled by a language gap, so he is in my class. He arrives with drywall dust in his hair and his mind filled with questions about American slang.

"What is this word 'pussy'?" he quietly asks me. "I do not understand. At work, they tell me, 'You are a pussy,' and then they yell at me, 'Hey, Cosmin, do you eat pussy?'"

During break time, Cosmin and I go outside, and he smokes a cigarette and drinks coffee while I explain the ways you can use the word "pussy." The moon is full, and we walk the half block to the river. "Pussy," I say, as I point to my crotch. I can tell Cosmin doesn't quite understand me, so I curl my right hand so my fingers make a tube and I push my left forefinger in and out of the tube, and I ask, "You know, this?" Cosmin nods his head up and down. I take my left forefinger and touch it to the opening of the tube and say, "pussy," "pussy," "pussy."

Cosmin spits his coffee, falls back, and laughs a bellowing, Romanian-accented laugh. I think to myself, I love my job. I know that I have broken through the drywall dust, fatigue, and pain, and he won't forget this word, and tomorrow on the job he will use it. Cosmin can now speak like a construction worker, a job he hates. He was a high-tech worker, educated, and middle-class in Romania. He is not coarse like his coworkers on the drywall crew.

Our class break has run too long, as usual, and so I leave Cosmin outside smoking his cigarette and wander back to the classroom, knowing that the students will coerce each other to come back to the classroom and once again start trying to speak English while still thinking in the patterns of their native languages.

It is early morning. I go outside, and I cannot even see a whisper of the coming sunrise as I look at the naked branches of huge, old cottonwoods in my neighborhood. I like to imagine their trunks as the legs of elephants frozen in the ground. I grab the newspaper, gauge the temperature, and go inside to prepare coffee. I move slowly in the morning—in a fog, disoriented, and aching. After breakfast, I pull on a patched pair of jeans over long underwear, and then my favorite ratty, '70s vintage wool sweater over my old canvas hunting shirt. Next, my forty-year-old down vest that has been given new life numerous times by restuffing it with down. For the outer layer, I grab a sweatshirt with JOHNSON DISPOSAL SERVICE emblazoned on the back. I like to wear this sweatshirt as an ironic joke when I am Dumpster diving to minimize interpersonal conflicts that might result in the police being called. Considering the number of times I've been contacted by the police this year, I think the ironic joke aspect of the sweatshirt is working better than the preventative aspect. I pull on a sturdy pair of hiking boots and duct-taped gloves, and I'm out the door.

Now it is a red morning. Wispy clouds lie low on the horizon; reds bleed into oranges, yellows, and then into the light bluish gray of morning. I can make out the corrugations in the bark of the old cottonwoods. They still look like elephant legs. It is cold, achingly cold, the type of cold where your body wants to shrivel back its exposed parts. This is my favorite time of day. A time when quiet reigns, even in this small city. The only loud noises are made by garbage trucks or by flights of geese venturing out for their morning feed. As I walk to the car, I can hear the snow crunch, step by step. I have been exploring meditation techniques for years in a selfish effort to slow my spinning mind, and it dawns on me that this could be a wonderful meditation. Doing nothing but walking and listing to the crunch of the snow under my feet.

Then I spoil the silence by starting my car. After traveling for perhaps eight blocks, I spy a roll-off. A roll-off is one of those very large Dumpsters you see at construction sites; it's called a "roll-off" because when it is set on site, it is simply rolled off a semitruck. This roll-off has numerous pieces of construction refuse sticking out of the top, which is enough to cause me to pull alongside it and investigate. I climb up on a stepladder I always carry with me and peer over the top edge. Inside is the usual mishmash of construction refuse, dominated by broken drywall, two-by-fours with nails sticking out of them, twisted steel studs interwoven with steel electrical conduit, and vinyl floor covering. Upon closer inspection, I notice that some of the two-by-fours are about four feet long and are made of clear-grained redwood, not a knot in any of them. The redwood used to be a backless bench attached to a wall, and the bench's legs are broken off. Then I understand. This was the deconstruction of a small shower in an office complex. Probably a shower for office workers who exercised at noon or rode their bikes to work, and the new employer has decided that such niceties are not necessary and they can get more efficiency out of the space by eliminating the showers. Not that this shower was ever used anyway, for the redwood looks as new as the day it came out of the mill. Hardly a drop of water has touched this redwood, and here the bench sits in a Dumpster. Refuse.

Straight-grained wood like this has to come from large trees. Large redwood trees mean virgin, old-growth trees that used to stand hundreds of feet tall in forests along the coastline of western North America. This redwood is the world's tallest tree and a keystone species of the redwood forest. I have been in redwood forests only a couple times in my life, and seeing them for the first time was equivalent to seeing the ocean. They are cathedrals of nature containing ferns taller than I stand, and banana slugs and sticky salamanders that teach every child not to touch them.

Now I'm angry. What kind of back-assward value system carelessly trashes *unused redwood*? I try to remember the efficiencies of scale justification an economist would give for trashing this redwood, but I have lost the ability to think this way.

There are two redwood benches, and the second of them is buried under some drywall and broken glass. So I sit on the edge of the Dumpster with my face turned to the sun and soak in the scene. My body has more than its fair share of old-age aches and pains, and I hope to minimize the damage, so I grab a warped eight-foot two-by-four and use it as a lever to pry up some broken drywall a few feet, anchor my end of the two-by-four, and then go about trying to wiggle loose the bench from the pile. "Patience," I tell myself, "patience." It won't come free, and my back is already telling me that I will pay for this tomorrow. Then I notice some fiber-optic cabling looped around the bench, holding it tight. I take out my knife and, while still pulling back on the redwood, cut the cable. Suddenly, I am on my butt hugging the redwood bench. I feel like a child hugging a stuffed toy and am almost that happy. With a little work, these will make beautiful redwood benches for my garden, or someone's sauna.

Yen is from Vietnam. She is young, probably about twenty-five, slender, and stylish, and she has long coal-black hair that frames her face. She is very pretty, almost sultry. She used to be a high school chemistry teacher in Vietnam. Her handle on spoken English is the worst in the class, but she is everyone's favorite because she is such an effusive and affectionate person. She cannot talk to another person without at least touching them, commonly hugging them. One time I was sitting, practicing pronunciation with Thomas. Thomas pronounced the word "ring," almost perfectly. Yen desperately struggles to pronounce this word, so I told her to come over and join Thomas and me. I then told her to sit in my seat, and with a big innocent smile on her face, she just sat in my lap. The class started whooping, and I felt the warmth of a reddening face sweep over me.

Yen has been in the United States four months. She is a mail-order bride. She works eleven to twelve hours per day at a nail salon, an illegal worker. Her American husband takes her earnings away from her and refuses to give her even a cent for an allowance. A couple weeks ago, Yen announced that she no longer had a ride to class, so she would have to quit. Her husband had decided that he was too busy to drive her to class. There is an inadequate bus system in our town, so she had no other options. Nowadays, my assistant, Donna, drives twenty miles out of her way to give Yen a ride to class and take her back home, twice a week. Donna works at the county health department and is well-versed in how much and what kind of violence is legally allowable. Donna asks Yen if her husband has hit her. She says no. We keep a close watch. Donna also picks up Rati. Nobody gives Rati shit. Donna says Rati spends part of the drive lecturing Yen on how a proper husband should act. We wait and we watch. I fear that the streets in America for Yen will be paved in bruises and not in gold.

I am a metal junkie. Unearthing the redwood exposes glass shower doors framed in extruded aluminum. I expend exorbitant amounts of physical energy in order to pull aluminum, copper, and stainless steel out of Dumpsters, especially aluminum. Every bit of it I can put back into the production stream is made back into new aluminum stock in a process that takes about one-twentieth of the energy that it takes to make aluminum from raw ore. And the icing on this piece of cake is that I earn forty-five cents for every pound of extruded aluminum I take to the scrap yard. What a deal! Save a few cubic feet from being torn from Mother Earth, save a bunch of energy, have a hoot of a good time. I get out a screwdriver, and I go to work dismantling the shower doors, taking time to strip off layers of clothing as the morning warms.

I move on and spy an apartment complex with teasers—bags and boxes overflowing the Dumpsters. Overflowing Dumpsters draws us scavengers faster than Subarus to a sustainability conference. I take an old ski pole—my diving stick—and walk over to the nearest Dumpster. I push around the multitudes of plastic trash sacks, cardboard boxes, and assorted other gooey refuse. I peer over the edge of the Dumpster and probe and push. When I poke a bag about halfway down, the ski tip transmits a telltale feeling. The bag feels solid. Your everyday household trash does not feel this way. It is composed of hard spots and empty spots with no continuity to the texture. I push again to make sure it's not the dreaded baby diaper bag—the smell of old diapers drives me out of a Dumpster faster than any other smell. This bag feels like it's full of leaves, clothing, or kitty litter. I push and lift a little; it's not kitty litter—a bag of litter is extremely dense compared to most household trash. I push again, and I can tell it's clothing. I stick the end of the ski pole through the looped handles and lift and drag the bag up over the rim of the Dumpster. I take a casual glance around the parking lot and then cut open the bag. The bag is a collection of clothing and assorted personal items. I hastily sort the clothing from the personal items; I'm a little paranoid on this subject. I have been stopped many times by the police when I'm digging in a Dumpster, and although they are generally disgusted by the thought of someone doing this, they do not prosecute me if I allow them to search my car and show them that I am not an identity thief. I am often given a lecture about how I should try to find something less disgusting to do with my spare time. I look at their big guns, think about how much I hate the idea of spending any time in jail, and politely tell them I will give their suggestion some serious thought. So I sort at the Dumpster. Later I may sort again. I make one pile to save for family, friends, students, and an eventual garage sale, and one pile for Goodwill Industries. I have fun, the people at the garage sale have fun, and the circle goes on.

In the "save" pile is a pair of Teva sandals. I check the soles for wear. The edges of the cleats on the heel are sharp with no rounding, definitely unworn or barely worn. Next comes a pair of Birkenstock clogs and three pairs of just-washed and folded jeans adorned with commercially made wear patterns. (Commercially made wear patterns, what a statement about our society, eh?) On top of the "save" pile are six or seven blouses with brand names like "Hanky-Panky," "Jodi Christopher," "Tickle Me," "Definitely," "Possessed," and a pair of sweatpants with the brand name "Big Flirt." No Gap or Old Navy for this gal, although I have certainly found hundreds of pieces of clothing sold by these two corporations. My ever-spinning mind wonders, after years of seeing items in the Dumpster, still usable and costing hundreds of dollars when new: don't parents today ever lecture their children about eating all their food because children are starving in other parts of the world? How ungodly rich and selfish are we Americans? When was it decided that having homemade patches on your jeans was not cool, while having factory made "distressed" jeans was? All I know is that sifting through the unwanted items of suburban Americans has alienated me from these faceless people whom I know quite a bit about, but thankfully I don't know who they are. I do know what parts of town they live in, and I also know that these parts are strongholds of the anti-immigrant sentiment that is so strong in America right now.

On Wednesday, I look down the hallway of our school's building, and I see an old student of mine whom I taught for numerous years, Sancho. Sancho worked as a "contractor" for a local firm that laid tile. In Mexico, Sancho was a computer programmer and hardware technician. He would usually show up to class late and very quietly slide into a chair. He always had just taken a shower and was wearing clean clothing. Sancho is in his mid-twenties, slim, very gentle, and quiet. When I first taught him three years ago, he knew absolutely no English, and now he is approaching fluency. He is residing in America illegally and wishes he did not have to be here. He has a three-and-a-half-year-old daughter whom he has not seen for over three years. He is from Mexico City, and his story is similar to many others. He crossed over the Arizona desert on foot in the winter. He said he could not imagine that the desert could get so cold. Everyone in his group huddled together at night in order to conserve heat, and when someone would show signs of losing consciousness, that person would be dressed in the others' thin clothing, placed in the middle of the group, and lain on to be kept warm.

Now, Sancho lives in a small house with six other men from Mexico. They are all from the same extended family. They all work ten to twelve hours a day, six days a week—seven if they could. If they have a day off on Sunday, they go to church, and then they watch soccer on TV and spend the day on their cell phones talking to families back in Mexico, which is where they send most of their money.

In my English as a Second Language class, we always talk about family, because that is an easy subject to use to teach language. All immigrants miss their families back in their home countries, but when Sancho talked about his wife and his children, the pain and longing was clearly expressed on his face, even if he did not have the English vocabulary to describe his feelings yet. I told Sancho to go home, that he would be much happier. Sancho just looked at me, and I could see my ignorance in his eyes.

For a couple semesters, Sancho had intermittent open sores on his fingertips and the palms of his hands, because his hands were exposed to caustic agents in the glue and grout used in tiling. I asked him about his hands because they horrified me. He told me that he had a pair of gloves, but they wore through, and he did not have time to go get another pair because he needed to finish his job quickly, otherwise the boss would yell at him. I said, "*El jefe?* You are a contractor to this company, so you really don't have a boss." Once again, Sancho looked at me, and I saw my ignorance reflected. So I introduced Sancho to Bag Balm, that wonderful curative substance used to protect the udders of cattle. It became a short-term conversation with us. He would show up with open sores, and I would say, "Bag Balm," and he would very quietly say, "Yes, yes." I offered to go and talk to his employer and demand that the employer hire him as a regular employee and offer them some benefits, but Sancho pleaded with me to not do that. "He treats me well," Sancho said, "I am happy to have a job at all." As I would teach, I would notice Sancho unconsciously touching the sores on his hands. On the backs of immigrants—that is how America was and is still being built.

These students are always extremely respectful, polite, hard-working, family oriented, and embarrassed at their lack of education. Sancho and a friend, Liborio, told me, "Tim, our schools are terrible, and so in America we are very embarrassed because not only do we not know the language, but we are uneducated. We want to be educated. We want to go to school, but we need to make money for our families first. We need to make sure that our children can go to school, so at least they can be educated. We do what we need to do, provide for our children, so maybe they may have a better life." How can I argue with this attitude? So when I check to see who has done their homework at the beginning of every class, and the Latinos have not finished theirs, I know the construction business is booming. If they have a day off because of inclement weather, then I am inundated with their homework.

I poke and probe with my dive stick until I hear the telltale noise of dishware or glasses or coffee cups making a *tink-tink* sound. I poke the tip of the ski pole through the bag this time and, catching it on the broken basket, pull the bag to me. This time I do a "cut and dump." I do this for two reasons. The first is that I can tell by the sounds coming from the bag that there may be lot of miscellaneous little kitchen or bath trinkets in this bag and this will be an easier method of finding them. Also, I have an interior alarm system that tells me when I have been hanging around a Dumpster too long and the chances of my being accosted by some well-meaning but misinformed individual (in my opinion) are high. So I slice the top of the bag open and dump its contents onto a broken plastic lid. I do this slowly, which allows me to stop pouring whenever I see an interesting piece of trash. I stop and sort numerous times. There are china plates, shot glasses, wineglasses (some broken and some not), spatulas, cooking ladles, a couple unopened boxes of pasta (yes, I will eat these), a knife sharpener, and a couple of aluminum pots. The aluminum pots have last night's meal encrusted on their surface. Another mystery of laziness that baffles me: the percentage of pots and pans that are thrown away because they have food encrusted on them is amazingly high. The very bottom of the bag is a mess of cords and electronic items. There are three cell phones, along with their chargers, an MP3 player that is apparently broken and that I can hopefully fix, and a calculator. I grab all the electronics. They are headed for my ever-growing pile of electronic items that resides in the corner of my barn.

The cell phones make me think of my friend, Cosmin. Repairing cell phones was his job in Romania. Has a single cell phone ever been repaired or fixed in the United States? I guess there is always a newer, better, flashier, trendier model for sale that we can't live without. For me, since I'm a metal junkie, I also know the long list of toxic compounds and heavy metals that are inside our electronic gadgets, especially cell phones. It is truly scary. I just keep on hoping that those rubber liners in our landfills hold for many generations, because I would hate to drink the water that drains through one of those landfills on its way to our municipal water supplies.

Finally, I glean the beer bottles from the top of the trash and put them into the recycling bin next to the Dumpster. I make a point of trying to practice compassion for other human beings, but it's tough when people can't be bothered to open a lid of a recycling bin, and instead toss their empty six-pack of microbrews into the Dumpster. If you recorded the sounds of me gleaning these bottles, you would hear a lot of glass clanking and my muttering, "Fucking assholes!" So I grab a six-pack at a time, open the bin's lid, turn the six-pack upside down, and shake (only glass goes in the bin) while muttering. Then I repeat this process until a level of hate and rage rises to a dangerous level, and then I quit. I grab my trusty dive pole and move on to another of the seemingly unending Dumpsters overflowing with plastic bags, cardboard boxes, and stinking, moldy leftovers.

I throw some Corona bottles in the recycle bin. Now I am thinking of my Mexican and Central American students. The immigrants I teach generally throw nothing away. I bring things from diving, and they gratefully accept whatever cast-off item I have, perhaps sending it back to family or giving it to other recently arrived immigrants. They ask me the same question everybody else asks me: "Where do you get all this stuff?" I answer that they are donations. When I am diving sometimes, I will see Latinos at the Dumpster, usually collecting aluminum cans, the currency of all outcasts. I always allow other divers their space; there are plenty of other Dumpsters. When I go to the scrap-metal yard, I see Guatemalan ladies who work for large catering services or hotels selling the aluminum food trays that the caterers use as throwaway items.

At times, it seems that all I can see are circles. Circles of reusing and recycling, obviously. But also circles of illegal immigration, circles of consumerism and the desperation of poverty, circles of sending the young and healthy north and sending back dollars in return. Circles of suburban homes and doctored papers and unwritten understandings. Everybody is telling lies—the immigrants, the employers, and the government—and these lies are passed in a circle, also.

So I keep putting the stepladder up, crawling over the lip of the Dumpster, and rescuing the unwanted items of suburbanites. I wonder why we give no thought to the depletion of resources, be it redwood, energy, metals, or human lives that are demanded by our consumption. I see this resource fallout on a weekly basis when I am in the bottom of the Dumpster and when I am teaching recently arrived immigrants, and I wonder when we will see how poor we have become.

My Father's Last Fortune

LAURA HENDRIE

Laura Hendrie was born and raised in and returned to Colorado. In addition to a book of interlocked stories, *Stygo*, about a failing company town on the prairies of southeastern Colorado, she has written a novel, *Remember Me*, about homelessness, memory loss, and embroidery in northern New Mexico. In this essay, she explains where she found the idea for her third book, *The Year We Won a Firebird*, which revolves around the gambling career of a family man in Colorado and the family who loved him.

Unless your parents die before you are old enough to understand that death is capable of taking them from you—which must feel for any young child as inexplicable as waking up one morning on an iceberg in the middle of the Antarctic Ocean—most of us after a certain age understand, intellectually at least, that dealing with the deaths of our parents is a natural part of life. It's something we're in all likelihood expected not only to face, but survive.

Perhaps this is why children who appear nearly immobilized by grief at the funeral of their mother or father can turn overnight into a group of gleaners as avid as shoppers at a Macy's basement sale. A house, a photograph, a coat, a favorite chair, a five-cent cigar ring— the sudden, grim need to dig up and count out and claim all that's left is not necessarily proof of avarice or selfishness, insensitivity or even love. It is only the child's determination to survive. To hunt through what death has left behind for what will continue. Something, *anything*. No wonder such bitter fights can break out over broken-backed books, used clothing, old furniture, bad paintings, incontinent pets, even appliances. No wonder the sibling who buys the Dior outfit and flies in from Europe for the funeral watches the distribution of the meager legacy with the same terrified, rapacious precision as her sister who wears rags from the Goodwill free box and hitchhikes to the service. And what of the parents who leave nothing behind? How are we to survive their loss if we don't have even a penny, a button, not even a straw of what managed to survive their death?

The answer is stories. However generous or stingy the material gleanings from a death may be, there are always stories, and these must be dug out after the ice storm and brushed off and carefully redistributed among those still living. Like cold-clumsy explorers divvying up the last of the supplies, the survivors must share the stories and choose which ones they need. They must flay each one and salt each one and cure each one in salt or smoke to make them last, and then they must pack all the stories up again and go on with the rest of their lives. This is what funerals are for—not only to gather as a family to grieve a death but to glean enough stories from each other to survive life.

If I was more aware of this than my sisters were eighteen years ago when our father died, it was because I had decided to write stories for a living. I'd found teachers who knew how to study stories and mentors who knew how to write them. I'd filled my house with glorious novels and my head with the power of language, and I'd surrounded myself with friends who were just as hungry as I was to write something good. After three years of gathering all the resources I thought could help me become a professional fiction writer, I had only one thing missing: stories.

There were plenty of them out there—as a writer with a capital "W" all but branded on my forehead, I couldn't stop long enough to eat a sandwich or tie my shoe without somebody saying "I have a good one for you"—but I needed stories that rose out of my own experience. Stories that could answer questions about where I'd come from and who I was and what I believed, stories I could dig into and rework until they turned into the same kind of believable fiction I loved most to read.

For stories like that, I realized, I had only one reliable resource. He was someone who knew nothing about fiction. The only reading he'd ever done were tout sheets, the only writing he sweated over were gambling IOUs, and the only stories he ever worked on were the ones he made up to explain why he shouldn't be in jail. He was, however, completely committed to being believable. In short, my father: the wiliest tale-teller of all, and perhaps the only person I'd ever known who had lived the art of invention as well as studied it—a fact I first realized as essential to my future on a snowy Christmas Eve night in 1990 when a policeman stopped by our house to say that at age sixty-seven, John Gibson Hendrie had been found dead of heart failure in an apartment next to a small racetrack a thousand miles away in Sun City, Arizona.

A few stories: By day, my father was an average, hardworking, shy, family-oriented, suburban businessman, but at night, anything could happen. Sometimes he came in the door with a bagful of cash he slammed on the kitchen table. If we were having difficulty making ends meet, he might show up with a Ping-Pong table, or a trampoline. Once, a truck from Indiana pulled up to our back door and dropped off a crate of ten thousand chopsticks for my mother. Another time, he came rushing in the house just as we were sitting down to TV dinners in the living room and yelled at us to get down on the floor. We had not seen or heard from him in over a week. *"Down, down!"* he yelled as he ran through the house flipping off the lights. There were four of us, and my mother was pregnant with a fifth, and she was not happy about being shoved off the couch in the dark. But he held her down, pleading with her to be quiet, and moments later, sure enough, a pair of headlights pulled up our circular driveway, paused ominously in front of our house and then moved slowly back out to the street.

Now, it may be true that he smelled like the tail end of a weeklong poker game, and that, in order to avoid a confrontation about his absence with our mother, he had paid a friend to pull into our driveway at the right moment to look like a thug—but to my sisters and me it didn't matter. When he told the story of how he had been hunted and robbed and pursued by a psychotic killer all the way to our front door, we were just glad he was still alive.

This is how I grew up, knowing there are two sides to every story. My mother's side—committed to the power of honesty, facts, and confession—and my father's side. He was committed to the power of the story. So was I. Just how committed I did not understand, but every time he started a story, my heart was in my throat over whether he would tell it well enough not only to soften my mother's anger but to convince us, despite what it looked like, how much he still loved us. And that is how I picked up his commitment to being believable, by seeing time and again how it could save a marriage and rescue love, but also what it demanded in terms of personal risk and faith and loss.

This became instantly clear the day we received the news of his death. He had been lying in his apartment for two days before they found him. My family sat through a stunned, silent Christmas, and the next morning my mother, my older sister, and I flew to Arizona to sign for his ashes, sell his car, and close up his apartment. On the plane, we decided my mother and sister would go straight from the airport to the mortician's office while I would go clean out his apartment. "Don't get sentimental," said my sister under

My family sat through a stunned, silent Christmas, and the next morning my mother, my older sister, and I flew to Arizona to sign for his ashes, sell his car, and close up his apartment.

her breath as we landed. "We don't have time to get sentimental. Just throw out everything."

I nodded. I planned to do no such thing. My father had died! A loss big enough to commit words to! Stories to! A career! I walked off that plane with an empty suitcase for his mementos and my pockets stuffed with writing paper, sweating with excitement and fear that I would miss something, or lose my nerve.

His apartment looked like this: a closet stuffed with brand-new polyester clothes the color of Easter, a bed, a table, a kitchenette, an orange plaid couch, a matching chair, a coffee table, and venetian blinds. No pictures on the walls. No souvenirs, no mementos, no knickknacks or certificates, no diaries or journals or books or lists next to the bed where he had died, no refrigerator magnets, no prizes. Nothing to glean that might be his. Nothing to show he'd even had a past, let alone a family. The only thing that made his apartment less anonymous than a motel suite at the airport was a wall of metal filing cabinets in the living room, which ran from floor to ceiling. These I attacked, refusing to be cowed by the size of the job. But it was hopeless. Every drawer was packed with gibberish. That is, instead of the meticulous notes I had hoped for about his marriage, his mistresses, his adventures, his narrow escapes, his passionate beliefs and fears, and his five kids, all I found were notes about horses, bets, and race results. Notes about the one thing I had failed since childhood to acknowledge as true: my father's commitment to gambling. And worse, every single word in those metal filing cabinet drawers had been written in code, a secret hieroglyphic system he had invented that none of us knew how to read.

At the end of that day, all the filing cabinets were empty, and everything he owned was in the Dumpster behind his apartment complex. The only thing I kept was a book, *Scarne's Complete Guide to Gambling*, inscribed by the author, whom my father had apparently played against. I had no intention of reading it. I took it only because I had learned in school to appreciate books inscribed by the author. I left shaken, empty, in despair. I had just cleaned out my dead father's apartment—how good a story can you get?—and I was about to return to writing school with absolutely nothing new to write about.

As I was pulling away in the rental car, I noticed a group of white-haired, sun-withered, bony old men in pastel-colored polyester clothes around the Dumpster. Some of them had crawled inside the Dumpster to stand on top of the trash. They were going through what I'd thrown away. Some looked confused, but some were scooping up armfuls of pages and passing them over the top of the Dumpster to other men. It was a last troubling memory of that day for me: all those strangers so greedily scavenging my father's work for clues, while I, the daughter in search of a legacy, was leaving with an empty suitcase to face the blank page in my typewriter.

But no matter how many ideas you toss away, the good ones will find their way back. Twenty years after I left all proof of my father's commitment to believability in that Dumpster, my literary agent called to inform me that my publisher wanted me to write a letter of introduction about myself for my next book. Such was the price, he explained, of living in the age of celebrity authors. "Just introduce yourself, say a little something about why you wrote the novel, and be funny."

Funny?

I was furious. I'd written a whole novel, and now they needed me to write some kind of memoir to go with it? What more did they want, a pound of flesh? I decided to give them a joke. Something truthful, yes—but something they would never be able to decipher. I'd tell them about my father. I'd be funny and tell the truth—but it would not be the truth about me. It would not be about how I wrote my novel or how I learned to write or what I would write next, and it would not, NOT include even a hint of my personal beliefs, which seemed to me nobody's business but mine.

But, as E.M. Forster once said, "How do I know what I think until I see what I say?" and that is the truth. By the time I finished my little joke, I had discovered that by telling one of my father's favorite stories, I had learned not only why I wrote the last book but how I would write the next. And I had also gotten a glimpse of where my commitment to believable storytelling had come from and where I could go to find more.

Here then is the letter I wrote. It's short. And it's all true.

Dear Nat,

Since you asked me to explain where my novel *Remember Me* comes from, I'd have to say that though he isn't alive, isn't in the book, didn't read much, and wasn't a writer, my father is as much to blame as anyone. He believed in legitimacy as well honesty, and to prove it he started five legitimate businesses at the same time: the Red Hendrie Swimming Pool Co., The Red Hendrie Sauna Co., the Red Hendrie Hydroponics Greenhouse Co., Red Hendrie French Bidets, and Red Hendrie Bomb Shelters, Inc. But his true calling was gambling. My father was a professional gambler. When I was growing up, he was so good at card counting he got himself banned from every casino in Las Vegas— which is why, when we needed money, he'd leave home with his hair dyed a different color or wearing a fake beard so the casino owners wouldn't recognize him. Sometimes they did, and, after congratulating him on his disguise, they'd hand him his coat, spin him around, and aim him back out the door before he'd even sat down to play. But this never really bothered my father, because as much as he liked bringing home money, he also liked bringing home stories. Big stories. After my mother made him promise to quit gambling, his stories about his card games grew enormous.

One morning, for instance, he went off in our station wagon and returned eight days later in a new gold Firebird convertible with a white leather interior. "Thank God!" he cried, collapsing in a heap on the steps until we came out to help him inside where my mother was fuming in the kitchen. I can't begin to do that story justice, but it included a mansion guarded by wolfhounds and a gang of Sicilians who expected free lessons in poker. My father explained how after three days at gunpoint, three *terrible* days of being forced to play cards for his life with a bunch of losers—when he suddenly realized he wasn't going to be allowed to even *call* my mother to wish her happy birthday—that was the end of playing nice. Hence, the Firebird, which he instructed my mother to park behind the house so that if the Sicilians came to our neighborhood looking for revenge, or worse, another game, they wouldn't know which house was ours.

I remember watching my mother listening. Standing with her back to the stove, arms wrapped around herself with a cigarette in one hand. She was still in her bathrobe and her hair was furred up in the back like an electrical charge had gone through it, and when my father finished his story, beaming with pride, she stubbed out her cigarette and left the room.

On the other hand, she must have believed *some* of it, because she never left that Firebird parked out in front of our house, either.

Which is probably why I write the way I do. It's not that I haven't had interesting experiences. I've been a firefighter, a chainsaw crew leader, a vaudeville theater waitress, a disc jockey, a law enforcement officer, a ditch digger, a bartender, a painter, a stone yard manager, a 911 radio dispatcher, and a bomb shelter saleswoman; but I have yet to find much there worth writing about. Indeed, I don't want to deal out dull facts—I want to burst in the door like my dad used to do, with a great wad of cash and a wild story about how it happened. That's what makes writing fun, when the stakes are high enough to make the bluff worth a shot. So no, Nat, though I do live in a small mountain town in New Mexico, similar to the town I described in my novel, I can still say that I wrote *Remember Me* without worrying much about the truth. I worry about telling the story. And that's alright, because I've discovered that when I believe a story, really *believe* it, I usually end up with the truth anyway. That's how my dad ended up driving a gold Firebird off to his next poker game. And as far I'm concerned, that's enough truth for *any* storyteller.

Handprints in the Canyon

ANDREW GULLIFORD

Andrew Gulliford began his teaching career in Silt, Colorado, where he taught fourth grade and where bumper stickers read "SILT HAPPENS." His house there has a garage gleaned and built from railroad ties, telephone poles, and adobe. He likes to glean and save vintage American cars, and his best find was a 1953 Buick woody station wagon found on the Mexican border with flat tires, locked brakes, and a rusted engine. Dr. Gulliford is now a professor of Southwest and American Indian Studies and History at Fort Lewis College in Durango, Colorado. Living in the Four Corners area, he continues to glean from five thousand years of human habitation in one of the most archaeologically and ecologically diverse landscapes in America. His photos, included in this book, can be seen at gullifordstravels.com.

The shadows grew long, and I knew I had to get off the slickrock and out of the canyon soon, or I'd never cross the wash in the proper place, find my way through the mud and the tangle of tamarisks, and climb up the other side to my truck. The shadows lengthened. Impatient and a bit depressed, I descended the canyon. I had been trying to glean some significant sign from the ancient inhabitants.

I'd spent a glorious spring afternoon high atop Comb Ridge, in the southeast section of Utah, breathing in the wind from far across the Navajo reservation and walking slowly, deliberately, to the top of the sixty-five-million-year-old uplift with Charlie, my Border collie mix. He eagerly led the way, tail up, nose down, eyes bright. We had napped close to the top of the Comb in sand beneath a juniper, and I'd seen a few small petroglyphs on the massive sandstone fins. I'd picked up a few pottery sherds and some red chert flakes, which I put back down on the ground and covered with a thin layer of dirt. I walked without maps, wanting to discover the landscape on my own.

The weather had been splendid, the temperature just right, perfect for hiking the Comb, but despite looking and searching, scanning the horizon and the cliff walls with my small birder's binoculars, I had not seen much of consequence. Of the dozens of Ancestral Puebloan sites along the Comb, I had found nothing special. I wanted to find a spectacular site that would reach out to me across time and space and jolt me out of the present, but no luck. I was tired, a little hungry, irritable, and late getting down to the truck. I hadn't gleaned anything from the landscape.

My hiking sticks had been clicking down the canyon floor as I moved quickly, looking for small barrel cactus, tree roots, and bends in the trail. The light was gone, and, though the air was not yet cool, night was coming. I approached a long, south-facing alcove. Suddenly, for no reason I can remember, I looked down at a low Basket Maker wall from more than a thousand years ago. The Basket Makers preceded the Anasazi (Ancestral Puebloans), and this site had been severely pothunted by vandals looking for bowls, baskets, anything. The desecration meant there were no standing ruins and no need to stop. And then I saw it. High up. Higher than I could reach.

What I saw rooted me to the spot. My blood pulsed through my upper body, and I heard it roar. As silence and shadow became darkness, I saw the row of exquisite handprints ochre red and fifteen feet high. I was not alone.

In the shadows I saw the red hands, large and small. A few yards away were more handprints, white this time around the edges, negative handprints made from paint held in a young man's mouth then blown against the wall by using a small reed tube. In this style of pictogram, the shape of the hand and each distinct finger was outlined in white—unlike the red prints where the hands had simply been dipped in ochre paint. I stood stunned, my dog burrowing into the sand, ready to spend the night.

I had not been stopped by a high cliff dwelling or an etched petroglyph, but rather by the simplicity and humanity of handprints waving to me across time, frozen forever in a moment of playfulness, asserting, "This is us. We are here. These are our hands."

Down canyon the stars came out one by one. The evening star appeared, and then the others shone. When I could see the handprints no more, I finally started walking, more slowly now, at peace. I did not worry about finding my way to the truck.

The Old Ones had been there. They would always be there. The subtlety and intimacy of the presence of the handprints in the canyon struck me more deeply than if I had stumbled upon an unknown cliff dwelling. Though they had been made a thousand years ago, the red and white hands, particularly the children's prints, reached across time and space to my heart.

I came out of the canyon into a brilliant rising moon. I was flush with warmth and affection for a people who had left their telltale sign in such careful, colorful patterns. I was humbled and grateful. My dog and I stepped off the steep bank into the mud and tamarisks as moonlight glinted on my truck's windshield above us and through the trees.

I had come down through the canyon too fast, in too much of a hurry, caught up in all the modern pettiness and busyness that burdens our lives. Had I not paused to study the handprints, I would have hit the arroyo in the deepest dark with no moon and stars to guide me. Despite my canine companion, we probably would have gotten lost. But with the moon on my windshield, I found my truck on the arroyo's opposite bank. What had drawn me to that alcove precisely when I needed to slow down and wait for the rising moon? What had made me look up at that exact moment? I'll never know, but in canyon country, as across the West, there are always secrets in the landscape, silent signs from those who went before. There are messages from the past to the present, and stories on stones.

Wallace Stegner wrote, "Describing a place, we inevitably describe the marks human beings have put upon a place, the uses they have put it to, the things they have been taught by it." To describe human history and the West, Stegner notes, "is quaintly begun in the completely human impulse to immortalize oneself by painting or pecking or carving one's private mark, the symbol of one's incorrigible identity, on rocks and trees."

Writing about Dinosaur National Monument in northeast Utah and northwest Colorado, Stegner described Fremont culture archaeological sites. He chronicled remote habitation sites of these northern Anasazi cousins along the Green and Yampa rivers, "and—most wistful and most human of all—the painted hand prints and footprints, the personal tracks that said, and still say: 'I am.'"

Across the vastness of southwestern deserts, on unnamed mesas on the Colorado Plateau, or in mountain meadows beneath Rocky Mountain peaks are traces of human presence over ten thousand years. Rocky Mountain National Park has prehistoric Ute Indian game-drive fences of brush and stone used to herd mountain sheep into ravines where they could be killed by atlatls and bows and arrows. The remnants of Ute pinon-juniper wickiups and tree platforms exist on the Uncompahgre Plateau on Colorado's Western Slope and in the White River National Forest.

In Yellowstone National Park, a dozen wooden war lodges remain deeply hidden in the backcountry. Within the center of the Bighorn Medicine Wheel atop Medicine Mountain in central Wyoming are horseshoe-shaped vision quest circles within the 1,500-year-old wheel. Far to the south are Pueblo shrines and harradura stone placements for leaving offerings and paho sticks.

Along the base of Comb Ridge are old forked-stick Navajo hogans, facing east. Everywhere in the West, signs—silent, subtle, significant—can be gleaned from the landscape not from a far perspective, but from walking slowly and coming to know the creeks and canyons, sandstone ledges, and trails through tall timber.

Prehistoric painted hands in southwestern canyons evolved in time into historic inscriptions as fur trappers, scouts, ranchers, and settlers moved across the West, for Native Americans are not the only ones who left their marks upon the western landscape. Anglo pioneers did, too, and their marks were often initials, dates, inscriptions—anything to mark their passing through the mountains and canyons of the West. Handprints became dates, initials, full names, and finally flowering phrases etched into soft stone. At El Morro National Monument in New Mexico, Spanish conquistadors left their inscriptions south of the Zuni Mountains. For three hundred years, priests, soldiers, and explorers left their names on Inscription Rock at El Morro. In Spanish, they wrote of their travels, including the 1605 carving: "*Paso por aqui el adelantado Don Juan de Onate del descrubrimiento de la mar del sur a 16 de Abril de 1605*" (in English, "Passed by here the Governor Don Juan de Onate, from the discovery of the Sea of the South on the sixteenth of April, 1605"), meaning the discovery of the Gulf of California.

Two centuries later, the homeward bound Captain William Clark left his name and the date 1806 along the Yellowstone River, where it can be seen on the sandstone butte he christened "Pompeys Pillar." But fur trapper William Ashley's 1825 inscription along the Green River was flooded under Flaming Gorge Dam. As settlers crossed the landscape beneath towering summer cumulus clouds, they left their names, dates, and plaintive complaints or exultations on the Oregon Trail at Scott's Bluff, Nebraska, and along the Sweet-water in Wyoming.

Writing about western inscriptions, James Knipmeyer notes, "In the Colorado Plateau region I have found them lightly scratched, with perhaps a knifepoint or horseshoe nail, pecked in with some sort of metal tool, possibly a miner's pick, and sometimes carved deeply with a chisel. Some have been painted with an actual pigment, but most of this type have been made with axle-grease from a wagon, wet charcoal, a fire blackened stick, or even the lead of a bullet." Knipmeyer adds, "But all of them proclaim to the world in one form or another that 'I was here. I am a part of history.'"

All of these types of marks, inscriptions, or modifications to the landscape are human ways of showing "we were here." In the vastness of the West, humans have always left their marks.

In the eighteenth and nineteenth centuries, explorers and settlers carved on stone. In the twentieth century, the impulse to leave a mark continued with Hispanic herders who brought thousands of sheep into high-country meadows and valleys. As the sheep bedded down in aspen groves, herders carved everything from horses, pistols, and self-portraits, to profiles of women they longed for.

Imagine being an artist working alone in a grove of shimmering white aspens carving a portrait that you will never see. A full decade will pass before the design will appear, subtle, serene. As a skilled calligrapher drawing on parchment makes a quick stroke, the Hispanic carver leaves the gentlest mark for the tree to embrace. As the aspen grows, the bark expands and the art appears like magic, but the artist never sees his work. Now, half a century later, the sheepherders are gone, and soon the trees will fall, too.

Deep in southwestern forests, beneath barren ridges but above the sides of creeks, stand aspen groves, some a century old. Among these smooth trees at the edge of mountain meadows can be found thousands of carvings etched by sheepherders who passed through the groves beside their bleating sheep. Carving symbols on trees, known as arborglyphs or dendroglyphs, is a revered tradition among high-country herders. A type of male occupational folklore, this cultural tradition is vanishing along with the trees themselves, lost to drought, blight, and other unknown impacts that are decimating the West's aspen forests. The issue is acute for Colorado, which grows half of the aspen trees in the Rocky Mountain states.

Aspen trees tell stories. When we read the trees, we glean a new understanding about the lost and lonely life of Basque and Hispanic herders, some from the Pyrenees in Spain and others from northern New Mexican villages. Among thousands of square miles on the Colorado Plateau, certain sections of aspen groves are literally covered with aspen art. In special places, herders and cowboys left messages for their companeros and created a sense of community.

On the Pine-Piedra Stock Driveway at Beaver Meadows and Moonlick Park in the San Juan National Forest, where the trail begins to climb at the ecotone boundary between aspen and fir trees, the carving becomes profuse. Names on the trees include Trujillo, Montoya, Bates, Isgar, Aragon, Archuleta, Gonzalez, Sanchez, Jacquez, and Valdez. Herders bringing sheep from one grazing area to another and back again as the seasons changed moved north from Ignacio, Colorado, along Spring Creek on the edge of the HD Mountains and up Yellowjacket Pass to Moonlick Park. They spent a few days resting sheep in the park, and, as the light played upon the aspen groves, they left their marks. Inscriptions include the poignant "Thanks to God" and the high-country haikuesque verse by cowboy Jim Bates: "NO LUCK, DAMN HORSES GONE! SNOW WALKING OUT DAMN!"

Decades-old calligraphy inscriptions nestle among the aspens clawed by bears and rubbed by elk antlers. Proud of their literacy and the ability to write their names, herders carved who they were, where they were from, and the date they carved the tree so that other herders would know of them. Some herders added a subsequent date each succeeding year they herded to explain to anyone who read the trees that they had returned. Rival herders occasionally vandalized each other's names.

In the Coconino Forest near Flagstaff, Arizona, herders brought sheep north from the deserts in the spring and returned them in late fall. In the San Juan Forest in southwest Colorado, Hispanic herders came from southern Colorado and northern New Mexico. By the early 1920s, Basque herders had arrived in the Coconino Forest from Europe. Post–WWII herders came from Mexico and Central and South America, and they do so to this day.

Carving categories included inscriptions; portraits of males with heads in profile and females from a frontal view; religious art (such as crucifixes and churches); poems; political slogans; and artistic expressions of mermaids, rifles, burros, sheep, maps, a flying saucer, and even a lifelike Elvis. Women were depicted artistically. "Aspen porn" became a significant subset as "a cultural form of expression" set back in groves "almost like a private gallery," notes archaeologist Linda Farnsworth, whose favorite glyph reads, "*VIDA INFERNAL, MAL VITAS SEAN LAS BORREGAS*" (in English, "INFERNAL LIFE, CURSED BY THE FEMALE SHEEP"). One memorable contemporary carving is of a female forest ranger complete with badge and braids.

The key to finding aspen carvings is to know the route herders took through the forest. In the 1940s, these traditional routes were marked with yellow signs stating "stock driveways" to help herders who may have varied from year to year. Some of those signs can still be found.

On the Groundhog Trail near Dunton, Colorado, carvers competed not only to leave their name and date but to do so in exquisitely fine penmanship as they carved the smooth skin of the aspens. The best carvers used a light touch, a lover's touch, to caress the trees as they remembered caressing their women so many months ago and miles away. Decades later, the herders' flourishes stand out in vivid, beautiful detail. The best carvers never gouged or cut but rather made gentle scratches, pinpricks with the sharp point of a knife, and their ephemeral art lingers upon trees beginning to age and die.

The best carvers used a light touch, a lover's touch, to caress the trees as they remembered caressing their women so many months ago and miles away. Decades later, the herders' flourishes stand out in vivid, beautiful detail.

This technique is one of the primary distinctions between historic aspen art and contemporary graffiti, which, because of brutal gouges, can damage and even destroy trees. The ethic now for all forest campers and hikers should be to "leave no trace" and leave the trees alone.

In the summer of 1955, New Mexican Joe R. Martinez was one of the best carvers. Folk art is generally anonymous and speaks to members of a select community or group, but Joe's style was unique and can be seen in marvelously simple cowboys with hats, women with hats, nudes, and other tableau. He was good, and he signed his work. On July 2, 1955, he carved one of the most amazing images in the forest. A woman in profile wears a fancy feathered hat, and below her, at the level of her chin, another woman appears, this one a crone. Is this La Llorona in an amazing double portrait?

Is this a herder's version of the beautiful Hispanic seductress who lures men with her body but who is really a witch?

According to Linda Farnsworth, statistical analysis reveals that 75 percent of the carvings were inscriptions with names or initials, hometowns, and dates; 5 percent were phrases or comments; and 20 percent were drawings in the categories of nature, buildings, portraits, guns, symbols—including crosses and hands—and erotica—such as images of "Venus of the Forest." Who knows how many carvings are yet to be found? With a light touch and a sharp knife, how many forest folk artists etched images as yet undiscovered?

As the sheep bedded down for the night, shepherds carved. Now fewer and fewer bands of sheep munch on forest grasses, and the herding tradition is declining as are stands of older aspens. Most of the men are gone now. They went back to their villages and small towns. On winter nights sitting in small kitchens, coffee in hand, they must have looked out their windows and thought of their trees—white in the moonlight, soft and silky to touch, silent except for the rhythmic rustling of leaves. They remembered the incessant bleating of their sheep and the way a herd moves through the forest slowly in a meadow and faster through the trees like a river flowing around rocks. The herders remembered their quiet evenings smoking, carving, and dreaming of home. The trees remember. Now we must read the trees to glean and understand a western tradition that's almost gone.

Painted handprints, rock art, and inscriptions carved into cliffs and trees all represent humans engaged in the western landscape trying to leave messages about having been there, having passed by, having seen and observed and left a small mark and knowing that in time the paint would flake, the inscriptions become weathered, and the trees fall. Historic inscriptions and aspen tree carvings are about a sense of place in the West and seeking an identity in a landscape ever changing, ever emerging. But there are also those marks upon the land that go beyond self and seek a communion with other purposes, other powers.

Shrines and pilgrimage sites remain, some centuries old for Native Americans, and at the sites of car wrecks are scattered descansos or crosses left along highway rights-of-way, small shrines to honor the dead. Brian Doyle, in *High Country News,* writes, "I mark the spots where girls and boys and infants and women and men have died along the roads, the naked white crosses, the flowers and flags. Once, in these spots, something left the earth." He adds, "The words we have are so thin. Life, soul, the miraculous energy that drives bone and meat toward love and light, the electric prayer of her, the hymn of him: gone."

As one moves across the mystical West, it is important to say a prayer, leave an offering, think of others. The Spanish phrase is *vaya con dios* or "go with God." North of Abiquiu, New Mexico, is a roadside shrine with a statue of the Virgin Mary. She is in a small stone grotto surrounded by offerings of rosaries, necklaces, full beer bottles, coins, and children's small toys all weathering in the wind and snow.

As I drive east up and out of the San Luis Valley toward the Spanish Peaks (or the Breasts of the Earth—in Spanish, "La Huajatolla," and in Ute, "Wahatoya"), I am looking for another shrine that I found years ago along U.S. Highway 160 somewhere west of Walsenburg. I remember this shrine because in those old days of driving slow-moving VW buses, the wind whipped my bus back and forth and I hung on to that big, black steering wheel for life. (Sooner or later the tie rod ends would give out, but that's another story.)

I took a photograph twenty-five years ago. Now it's a somewhat faded slide, but it's an image of the Virgin Mary in a stone grotto, brilliantly lit by late afternoon light. White beads grace her neck, and her arms are outstretched south toward the Breasts of the Earth and even farther south toward Mexico, the homeland of so many wanderers across the West. Now as I drive the highway thinking of my own journeys, my comings and goings between mountains and mesas, cliffs and canyons, I wonder if the shrine still exists or if some highway official has ordered it removed.

As I come up and over a rise, having sailed down La Veta Pass, I am struck again by the beauty of the Spanish Peaks and the cultural persistence of American Indians, Hispanics, and Anglos in this fabled landscape of success and sorrow. I begin to despair of seeing the shrine, and I assume that it has disappeared like so many other "roadside attractions" as the Old West has evolved into the New West and now the Next West of empty second homes and aging baby boomers.

Extractive industries of mining, lumbering, and cattle ranching have become silhouetted backdrops for eco-tourism, fly fishing, and mountain biking as the lycra- and polyester-clad legions sally forth from urban centers to explore the hinterland. The rest of us try to make a living in a mountain West now dominated by retirees who are modem cowboys and equity émigrés living on incomes derived far from the mountains and the mesas that we love. They get to retire while our children get minimum wages and the inevitability of high-priced housing.

For retirees and wealthy New Westerners, their marks upon the land are trophy ranches and huge, ugly ranch gates that proclaim the size of their egos and their wallets. As they say in Texas, "The bigger the gate, the smaller the place." No local in their right mind would build such gigantic eyesores, but newcomers are always erecting large log paeans to prosperity and private property. One entrance to an exclusive development north of Durango named "Two Dogs" has stylized barbed wire gates shaped like gigantic tennis rackets big enough to whack a moving van. They say in western Colorado, "The newer the neighbor, the bigger the gate," and they're usually right.

In the mountain west, locals build fences out of used skis. Rusted pickup trucks beside a barn are not so much junk as yard art. But New West newcomers don't like our old ways and the manner in which, with signs and symbols, we've fit into the landscape with humor and grace and maybe a rural mailbox placed upon an old plow or welded to a milk can set in concrete.

As I muse upon historical change and marvel at the Breasts of the Earth, I suddenly see the shrine. After all these years, it's still there. I pull over to the north side of the highway and see that time has only increased the shrine's pull and power. Now there are large wooden crosses in front of the grotto and dozens of offerings left upon the four-strand barbed wire highway fence. The large crosses are made of landscape timbers and railroad ties. Smaller crosses, merely two cottonwood sticks affixed with wire, are hung up and down the fence along with rosaries, faded plastic flowers, key rings, gloves, belts, strands of hair, toy bears, and small plastic U.S. flags. There are high school ID tags, crushed cans, coins, baseball caps, pine needle boughs, Christmas ornaments, and teething rings. On the ground, a simple cross of stones lies imbedded in the soft earth. The Virgin Mary is still there, still wearing the same white plastic beads, though now she has more necklaces, and her blue dress and cloak have faded to gray.

Charms of all sorts line the fence, which is covered with boots and shoes, fishing lures, and macramé. Socks and T-shirts blow in the wind like Tibetan prayer flags, but Mary stands serene where she has stood for decades, smiling upon the simple offerings left by the faithful in an ancient response, a folk response, to travel and travail and the need to say and leave prayers as we traverse the western landscape. The crosses and the offerings are a testament to faith and the need to be humble and count our blessings. Her outstretched arms receive us all. As small wooden crosses turn and twist in the wind, I am amazed at the power of place, the resilience of cultures.

I slowly scan the grotto before leaving, and I see something I've never seen before. In the recesses now in shadow, on both sides of the Virgin's statue, there are rock art petroglyphs carved into the low sandstone walls. Now I see pictograms, small painted images on the back of the stone grotto, and I know that this Hispanic shrine was also a special place for Utes and Comanches and other peoples traveling at the base of La Wahatoya centuries, perhaps millennia, ago. As I pull my cap tightly down against the wind, I am refreshed, rewarded for having slowed and stopped, having made my own pilgrimage to this roadside shrine.

I look again, this time for prehistoric painted hands, but the shadows are deepening and I have miles to go before I sleep. I turn away, but, like so many pilgrims before me, I'll return to look again for handprints, for signs upon the landscape, to glean a sense of place.

Things the Color of Stone

JACK COLLOM

Jack Collom joined the United States Air Force during the Korean War and wrote his first poems in Tripoli, Libya. He earned an MA in English on the GI Bill and has taught creative writing for over thirty years. He currently teaches Ecology Literature and Writing Outreach at Naropa University. Collom is the author of twenty-one books and chapbooks of poetry and three CDs (with musicians Ken Bernstein and Dan Hankin) and is responsible for three collections (with essays and commentary) of writings by children, all published by Teachers & Writers Collaborative in New York. His latest books are *Extremes and Balances* and *Exchanges of Earth & Sky*. He has twice been awarded a National Endowment for the Arts Poetry Fellowship. A "Day" was recently celebrated for him in his longtime home, Boulder, Colorado.

I get kids to create on paper. For over thirty years, I've made my living mainly by working with children of all ages as a poet-in-the-schools, and, as a lifelong birder and woods-walker, I sneak nature into the mix as often as I can. I find that virtually all writing ideas are good for facilitating nature writing. The shapes and energies of nature are inescapable, even in our most artificial constructs—the process of writing itself breaks down into the most homely and basic particulars in your life.

But one Earth Day in the 1980s, I was headed for an elementary school and wanted the students to respond more directly to the idea of Nature. I thought of having them write poems based on "Things to Save." First, I spoke briefly to the kids of list poems; catalogues have been a common element of both poetry and practical life for millennia. Lists are packed with information, and they encourage students to go in for surprise, to play with odd or far-ranging juxtapositions. Such poems tend to be rhythmic and energetic.

Then, very briefly (not wanting to preach), I mentioned the great eco-problems facing the world. Next, I asked the students if there was any nature in their classroom, and at first some pointed to the token potted plant; then someone called out, "Me!" and we proceeded to the wood and sand and oil behind virtually everything in the room.

I suggested that they needn't feel restricted to absolutely wild entities for their things to save; they could include little sisters, books, or the teddy bear with a missing arm and one eye pulled out on a rusty spring. Nature and civilization are entirely interconnected.

I also urged detail in the writing. "Don't simply save trees, animals, and water; save the lopsided old sycamore just south of Salt Creek, where the hermit thrushes sing." It takes imagination to see what's in front of you, to go beyond labels. I also tried to show the students that it's both fun and necessary to create variety in their writings—a biodiversity of savings. And I told them to vary the syntax in their pieces: to *talk* about their cherishable things.

I've used this idea over and over and across time have gleaned a huge selection of "Things to Save" pieces by young students. One thing that shines through these works for me is that poetry is a gleaning process, language and thought likewise. To glean is to pick things out from a great array, to seize upon certain possibilities, thereby gathering them to a new mix. To round up, amass, focus, rally, combine. Certainly, collage is a gleaning process. To list is to glean. Asking students to write "things to save" leads quite obviously to gleaning, of memory as well as imagination, and it cultivates an attitude favoring gleaning from the natural world—pulling whatever we pull with an eye for the greatest possible conservation.

Here are some of my favorite poems, all of them titled "Things to Save":

The darkness of shadow-like wolves
darting across the night like
black bullets, and the moon
shimmering like a sphere of glowing mass.
Let us save lush grass, green as green
can be, but, best of all,
imagination flowing with joy aha,
images it is composed of, it is this
that is making the earth grow
with flavor and destination.

Fletcher Williams, fifth grade

I'd like to save the sweet chocolaty chewy candy bars
that melt in your mouth, the warm cozy pillow that you
can't wait to sleep on, I'd like to save green meadows
that you run barefoot across running and running until
you collapse on the wet soft grass, the hot days when
you try to eat ice cream but it melts and plops on your
foot, I'd like to save the amusement parks where you go
on a twisty ride and throw up all over yourself but that's
just what you thought would happen, I'd like to save the
little green bug my big brother viciously killed six
months ago, I'd like to save the world all green and blue
and beautiful, I'd like to save the little things that
everyone enjoys.

Juli Koski, fifth grade

I'd like to save green meadows that you run barefoot across running and running until you collapse on the wet soft grass.

Save the broken old slinky that rolls down the stairs.
Save the blue paintcan that spilled on the floor.
Save my orange journal where I hide my deepest secrets.
Save the best book, for me to read again.
Save Br'er Rabbit, who steals carrots and cabbages and the
    hearts of children.
Save all the subtitles where I read of umbrellas.
Save all the canvases where Sonneborg put his
    masterpieces.
Save the cheeks of a child that go pink in the cold.
Save all the doors that keep us inside.
Save all the secrets that you whispered in my ear.
Save a great blue marble that is after all what this is about.

Helen Rhea V., eighth grade

Everything in the Universe.

The world.

Books that keep knowledge in them.

My friends Madison, Peyton and Mallory, I play catch-the-
butterfly with every day.

Passenger pigeons—they used to fill the sky but people
would shoot them down.

Daffodils in the green meadows.

The words that bring my mind to life.

My dog Rocket. His tail goes up. He plays with me, I try to
get the ball from him.

    I want to save my jack-in-the-box and red-and-black
    bike, my CD player, my sister's tricycle, and my
    apple tree and my pumpkin.

I want to save my cat Jimbo. He's 90 or 60 years old. He
has a raccoon tail

I want to save fir trees, bluish-greenish. They have roots.

I want to save my cat. She's brown. Her name is Zelda. We
keep her inside. She's sorta fast.

    I like the maple trees that grow.

I wish that brown recluse spiders weren't so poisonous.

I would like to save the earth, moon and stars. The moon
turns from a circle to a half a circle.

    The stars look like little dots.

I would save the tree they cut down last year except they
cut it down.

I love the whistling water.

I'd like to save the nice cool ice cream you eat on a hot day
  to make you cooler.

I want to save Emperor penguins 'cause they're good at
fishing and they look cool.

Save turtles. They look like a big green rock.

I'd like to play with my friends at the dawn of day . . .

                by the class (first and second grades)

Save pencils all riddled with teethmarks
where the writer has chewed out ideas gray
mornings shut inside at her desk and
Save all the tragedies and romantic
crayola sunsets people write about in love
poems,
Save the ice cream vendors in Manhattan
And the trees with cement as their soil, in Brooklyn
And especially save the gardens everywhere that
Giuliani thinks are such dangerous enemies
And Save the children, Save the schools,
Save the acronyms that lose themselves in
obscurity when an epoch, a decade, a
political era becomes obsolete; cut and dried
in a textbook that you can burn
for all I care
But Save the walk I took one day up
a path carpeted with wet leaves, among
damp-smelling life stored
in the red-like-a-rash, cracked, eroded,
shaming-the-empire-state-building tall trunks that make me
feel easily unneeded and out of place
Because, by the way, please don't save me.

Nell Geiser, high school

Save pearly everlasting dried broken at the roadside.
The sounds of Arenal at night. Lava
and parakeets in flocks, and storms.
Save hills and high cliffs, save
animal teeth, save
fur and claws and tendons and bones.
Save stars but change the constellations if you want.
Save baobab trees,
llamas, rusty old meat grinders,
the organ grinder's monkey. Save

old shoes and hair.
Save caterpillars, nasturtiums,
grass-of-parnassus.
Save chokecherries
and phosphorescence,
sea horses, flies.
Save stone walls for walking,
and drift wood on beaches.
Save things that live in the Indian Ocean.
and things that swim in the South China Seas.
Save sand.
Save music and humming and whistling through teeth.
Save people on streets, but don't save the streets.
Then sumacs, and fescue and fenugreek seeds,
and ladybugs, aphids, paper-birch, leaves.
Touch-me-nots. Cockroaches.
Carnivores. Herbivores. Omnivores. Fields. Save
seed shadows. Leaf litter. And marshes. Save
duff.
Sea shrimp and squid ink and
octopus feet, and
hurricanes. And 80-knot winds. And
sailboats thrown onto high cliff roads.
And slugs and snails and scallops and scarabs.
Kestrels and nightshades. Vipers and honey.
Save blue things. Save bower birds.
Devil's club, mulch.
Save sea otters, ospreys and
things the color of stone.

Saskia Wolsak, college

Hoş geldiniz, hoş bulduk

How Turkey Taught Me to Just Say Thanks

MICHELLE NIJHUIS

Michelle Nijhuis lives in a small town in western Colorado, where she gleans, skis, and writes about science and the environment. Her work appears in *High Country News, Smithsonian, The New York Times,* and many other publications, and she's the winner of several national journalism awards. But not long ago, she took a two-month break from both Colorado and journalism. The following essay recounts the results.

My house is plastered with mud, insulated with straw, and topped with solar panels. My floor came from an abandoned house, my doors from a salvage yard, and my mismatched windows from garage sales. My toilet is made from a five-gallon plastic bucket that must be emptied once a week, which is exactly as disgusting as it sounds. My car is ancient, my clothes are castoffs, and the wine I drink is very, very cheap.

I have my reasons. Because my husband, Jack, built our tiny house, our mortgage is nonexistent, and the bills we do have are few and small. Our low overhead shelters my writing career, and our lives have a threadbare, uncomplicated beauty that suits us

My house is plastered with mud, insulated with straw, and topped with solar panels. My floor came from an abandoned house, my doors from a salvage yard, and my mismatched windows from garage sales.

both. To me, the house, the toilet, and the bad wine have long meant freedom. The things others don't need, or don't want, are the things that have liberated me from obligation.

But before all this, before Jack and I met and married and started homesteading on a Colorado hilltop, Jack had another life. He spent much of his twenties living and traveling in Turkey, where he taught high school physics, guided yacht tours on the Mediterranean, and accumulated enough stories for a decade of dinner parties. When we first got married, we sometimes talked about going to Turkey together, but a trip to the other side of the world was an almost inconceivable extravagance.

Then, during a dark December weekend, Turkey came to us. Two friends from Jack's time as a tour guide brought us coffee and olive oil, stuffed us with peppers and savory beef, and demanded why Jack hadn't returned to visit. Had he forgotten them, forgotten his second home? We hesitated. Not enough money, we said. Too much work. They listened politely and then told us, in the nicest possible way, that we were being ridiculous.

We didn't change our minds immediately, but Turkey began to shimmer in our future. Before long, we were choosing a season and some dates, and, finally, we bought a pair of plane tickets, bank account be damned. We felt giddy and nervous, a couple of cheapskates on a sudden shopping spree. We didn't forget ourselves entirely; we planned to travel by bicycle and camp where we could. We would glean a trip from the unused and the unwanted, just as we gleaned our lives at home.

But of course, that's where things got complicated.

When Turks see a person doing something strange, they often extend their hands, rotating them as if fiddling with a stubborn combination lock, and raise their shoulders in an exaggerated shrug. "And just what the hell are *you* doing?" the gesture asks.

The first time I saw it, I asked myself the same question. We were pedaling slowly up a mountain pass in northeastern Turkey, just a handful of miles into our two-month trip, and I was battling both a headwind and culture shock.

We'd arrived in one of the most conservative parts of the country, where the Muslim call to prayer echoed through the cool alpine air, and headscarves were the norm for women. I was none too sure how my bare head and trousers would be received, and our haphazardly loaded bicycles only made us look more outlandish. It was no wonder, I thought sadly, that passing drivers were giving us the fiddly gesture.

But body language, it turned out, was just a substitute for friendly conversation. As we climbed higher and higher, we passed shepherds, construction workers, a teenager waiting for a bus. Each one motioned us over. "*Gel! Gel!*" they shouted. "Come! Who are you?" They offered us tiny glasses of hot tea, if they had them (they usually did), and plied us with questions about politics, religion, and, of course, what the hell we were doing. They often sent us on our way with a loaf of bread or a dollop of advice.

I loved the tea, and the enforced rest stops, but I had the distinct and unpleasant feeling I was eating other people's lunch. Jack sighed, in a tone I was beginning to recognize as half-irritated nostalgia. "You haven't seen anything yet," he said.

When we finally crested the pass, we began to search for a campsite, bickering over the options in the fading light. We saw a couple and their small son harvesting vegetables, and Jack stopped to talk with them. Yes, they assured us, the orchard we'd just passed was safe for camping; the owner lived far away, and wouldn't care anyway.

We found an inconspicuous spot under the apple trees and unrolled our tent, and within an hour we climbed gratefully into our sleeping bags. We were just dropping off to sleep when we heard a car approach, then rattle to a stop. Doors slammed. Great, I thought. Our first night on the road, and we're about to get hassled.

We lay still, listening.

"Chak! Chak!" said a tiny voice. "*Chak!*"

Jack laughed. The little boy from the garden had even remembered his name.

After a short foray into the darkness, Jack was back in the tent, carrying a plastic bag stuffed with bread and hunks of cheese. "They got worried about us," he reported.

I know that travelers, especially American travelers, are easily impressed by the hospitality of their foreign hosts. Everyone else on the planet, it seems, can make us feel more at home than our own neighbors. But I wonder if Turkish hospitality is a uniquely powerful force. Like so much else in Turkey, it's large, loud, and saturated with religion and politics. And it's completely unafraid of obligation.

In the days that followed, as we made our way toward the rainy Black Sea coast, strangers offered us countless glasses of tea, fed us extravagant meals, and insisted that we shower and sleep in their homes. A teahouse owner invited us to camp on the floor of his shop, and made us tea the next morning. We sometimes tried to refuse, eager to be as self-sufficient as we believed we were at home, but reluctance caused such consternation that we usually relented, glad for a hot meal and a few hours of conversation.

"There's a word for us," Jack said one evening.

"What? Moochers?"

"No," he said, laughing. "We're guests of Allah."

Muslim tradition was only part of the reason for our hosts' enthusiasm. Turkey, for millennia a global crossroads, is both European and Asian, Muslim and secular, ancient and newly born, and its multifaceted identity is confusing for Turks and foreigners alike. Turkishness, as a result, is a complex and fiercely guarded notion—and hospitality is one of its highest expressions.

One afternoon during our journey, we left the highway and pedaled up a winding side road, in search of a tenth-century Georgian cathedral. We admired the cathedral's ruined glory, then began scouting the small surrounding village for a camping spot.

One family offered us a space by the road, and we were setting up our tent when we heard a grumpy voice behind us.

"Who are you? What are you doing?" rasped a heavyset man in his sixties, thrusting two plastic bottles of Coke in our direction. Jack barely had time to introduce himself before the man began a long harangue. If Jack hadn't translated, I would have thought we were getting kicked out of town, but we were in fact receiving a very gruff invitation. "Come inside! You're staying with me! Bring your things!"

So we met the man we called the Hospitality Tyrant. The Tyrant and his wife lived for most of the year as a guest worker in Belgium, where the Tyrant was a foreman at a coal mine. They'd used some of their earnings to build a house in this isolated valley, where, unlike most of their neighbors, they enjoyed a flush toilet and running hot water. "Take a shower!" ordered the Tyrant, and when we meekly complied, we only perturbed him more. "You're done already? Those showers were too short!"

The Tyrant didn't like us much, and we didn't like him. But he was determined to uphold the pride of his estranged native country. When we left the next morning, stuffed with the enormous breakfast he'd ordered his wife to make, he said, "Now, you'd never get treated like that in America, would you?"

Turkish hospitality is often a political tool, and sometimes the politics are extremely local. Pakize, the owner of a small hotel where we stayed, carefully prepared a plate each morning for the garbage haulers on her street. "Drive-up service," she joked as she stood by her front window, waiting to hand breakfast treats to the crew in the passing truck. Payback wouldn't come immediately, but it was inevitable.

Even Turks themselves sometimes weary of the constant benevolence, and the bagful of expectations that comes with it. "So has everyone been telling you, '*Ye! Ye!* Eat! Eat!'?" asked Melek, a young woman who invited us to camp in her shady riverside yard. Bareheaded in a village where headscarves were nearly universal, she spoke of freedom and independence as enthusiastically as any

American college student. "I've had offers of marriage, but I'm too free for that," she said, twirling the fake wedding ring she wore to ward off curious men. But even as she set herself apart from Turkishness, and laughed about the excesses of Turkish hosts, she filled our plates to overflowing.

Weeks into our trip, I was still uneasy. I was used to independence, or at least the illusion of it; in Turkey, it seemed we accumulated debts with every passing instant, sometimes to people we couldn't stand. I worried that I'd traveled a very long way to take from others, often from people with far less than I had. I longed for the simplicity—and, let's admit it, the peaceful isolation—of living on castoffs.

In Colorado, I gathered the excesses of our affluent society because it saved money, because I hoped it did some good for the planet, and because it provided just about everything I needed. And because I took what others didn't need or want, I felt free. I didn't have to worry much about what and to whom I owed.

Turkish hospitality has the opposite intent. By encouraging everyone to give and take all they can, however and whenever they can, it tries to knit us all into a web of mutual and lasting obligation, of intricate, absorbing relationships. While this was lovely in theory, the reality made my introverted self crave a Dumpster to dive into.

But it also made me look at my own scavenged household with a critical eye. Under the glare of Turkish hospitality, the simplicity of my life at home started to look like loneliness, and its independence like snobbery. I suddenly felt tired of nibbling at the margins, of congratulating myself for taking up so little space. I realized I had a lot to learn from the Turks.

So bit by bit, I stopped fighting the forces of hospitality and started studying gratitude. I ate with enthusiasm and appreciation and reciprocated in whatever small ways I could. I brought gifts of food and flowers and used my tiny Turkish vocabulary to its limit. Jack, who had long ago remembered how to cope with hospitality, answered every question, and we offered as many stories as anyone was interested in. I was delighted and annoyed and embarrassed, sometimes all at the same time, but my days were never simple, and I was never lonely.

Toward the end of our trip, we and our bikes were caught in a rainstorm on the Aegean coast, buffeted by winds so strong they threatened to topple us. We stopped in a small village and asked directions to the teahouse, and in moments, we were stumbling through the doorway, frantically shedding our helmets and wet jackets. When we bothered to look around, we found ourselves at the head of a long, narrow room filled with tables, chairs, and groups of silent male customers. We were the focus of every eye.

We waited, and they waited. I expected them to make the fiddly what-the-hell-are-you-doing motion in unison. Finally, one man spoke up.

"Hoş geldiniz," he said—the traditional Turkish welcome. "Hoş bulduk," we responded. "We are pleased to be here."

"Hoş geldiniz," said the next man. "Hoş bulduk," we said obediently. And so it went around the room, each man solemnly welcoming us in his turn.

We pulled out chairs, asked for tea, and started rummaging in our packs for food. When we extracted a loaf of bread, someone appeared with a newspaper to rest it on. One man asked if we liked olives and produced a plastic bag filled with several pounds of oily black olives from his garden. Another customer placed a giant ripe tomato on our table, and someone else slipped us a folded paper filled with salt. We ate, Jack answered questions, they wished us luck, and we thanked them from the soles of our soggy shoes.

We ended our trip in Istanbul, in its exuberance of commerce and glamour, where the humble rituals of Turkish hospitality are drowned out by pushy carpet sellers. But even in the city's largest bazaars, bargaining is still accompanied by glasses of tea, and there's often a glimmer of genuine feeling on both sides.

On our last morning in Turkey, I set out alone to the gargantuan Blue Mosque, stepping around puddles from the previous night's rain. In less than twenty-four hours, I'd be home in Colorado, shoveling snow away from our dark, quiet little house. I knew I'd still live as cheaply as I could, but maybe I'd spend less time protecting my freedom, less time escaping entanglements. Maybe I'd spend more time grappling with the real junk around me, with the paradoxes of my own culture, my neighbors, and myself. Maybe I'd practice some Turkish hospitality.

I entered into the mosque's grand courtyard, which, on this early morning at the end of the tourist season, was almost completely deserted. A lone man with a broad broom was sweeping water from the stones, and he looked up and smiled.

"Welcome," he said.

"I was pleased to be here," I answered. I meant it more than I could say.

The Vanishing

CHRISTIE ASCHWANDEN

Christie Aschwanden's essays and articles have appeared in more than forty publications, including the *Los Angeles Times, Health, Skiing, Runner's World,* the *Washington Post, High Country News,* and *O, The Oprah Magazine.* She lives on a small farm in western Colorado in a house she and her husband are slowly remodeling with gleaned materials. She is a sucker for estate sales and, whenever possible, trades her fresh eggs, vegetables, and homemade jams to her neighbors for goat cheese, wine, and other handcrafted goods. She is the daughter of Ruth Friesen, who also has an essay in this collection.

The droopy sunflowers captured my eye. Most of the blooms in the painting stood perfectly ordered and upright, but two of them leaned over the vase, uncooperative. With its clumsy, thick brushstrokes and drab brown backdrop, the painting wasn't exactly beautiful, yet something about it beckoned me. I had recently moved into an old farmhouse, and after covering the laundry room in a fresh coat of yellow paint, I'd imagined myself painting a sunflower

I had recently moved into an old farmhouse, and after covering the laundry room in a fresh coat of yellow paint, I'd imagined myself painting a sunflower still life.

still life, much like this one, to hang on the wall. Except my painting would be bolder, brighter, and more graceful. It was all fantasy—I can't draw a circle, much less a sunflower—and even as I noted the painting's flaws, I recognized that it was infinitely better than anything I could have created myself. I pulled it aside.

I'd been riding my bicycle home from the grocery store when I stumbled upon an unfamiliar house with dozens of paintings strewn across the front yard. A sign in the driveway read "Estate Sale." I stopped.

At first glance, the paintings appeared to be scattered in haphazard clumps. But as I wandered about examining them, I realized that I was watching the artist's work evolve from one end of the lawn to the other. The sunflower painting, I decided, was an example of her early work. The composition was simple, a vase with sunflowers, and the uneven lines seemed characteristic of one just learning to wield a brush. Further along the grass lay another still life, this one a pastel depicting a green tea pot with matching cup and cream saucer sitting in the folds of a peach-toned tablecloth. The teapot bulged unnaturally on one side, and the perspective was a tad off, but the objects appeared more lifelike, the brushstrokes more sure and even than in the other works. A handwritten label on the back listed the painting's title, *High Tea,* and a price, seventy-five dollars, which had been crossed out and covered with the words "not for sale."

Moving down the line, I came upon a grouping of landscape paintings that showcased the artist's talents. There were dozens of them, depicting snowcapped mountains and red-rocked deserts that I recognized as the environs around our small western Colorado town. I identified a local peak behind a giant yellowing cottonwood tree that dominated one painting. The tree's trunk had long ago split near the base, and the artist had meticulously etched this detail with her brush, to show that this was not a fatal wound but a scar, a mark of life's capacity for survival.

As I contemplated the painting, a woman approached me. "I'll give you two for five dollars," she said. "They're not bad if you like that kind of folk art." Her tone told me that she didn't.

I asked her about the artist, who signed her work "B Hartford," occasionally with a tiny smiley-face flourish. Betty Hartford was her mother-in-law, the woman told me. She explained that what I had taken as Betty's artistic journey from novice to master had actually run in reverse, marking her descent into Alzheimer's disease. As I rifled through her life's work, Betty Hartford was resting, unaware, in a nearby nursing facility.

The news sparked a longing in me. Here was a woman's life, told in pictures. Betty wasn't dead yet, but already bits of her were being auctioned off to anyone who would take them. I cringed to think that someday my own life's work—my articles and essays and the books I hoped to write—might become leftovers at a garage sale. I left with five of Betty's paintings.

The one in my office, *Indian Summer,* depicts an early fall scene in the Rocky Mountains. The aspens have turned to gold, and the crag in the background is dusted with snow. When I first brought the painting home, I couldn't commit myself to hanging it on the wall. I liked it well enough, but I also knew that it wasn't haute art. It had a certain amateurish quality, like one of those formulaic paintings produced in thirty minutes on public television, and I wasn't sure it warranted prime wall space. So I set it atop a book-shelf facing my desk.

I look at the painting every day, sometimes as I try to gather my thoughts or find the perfect word for whatever I'm writing about just then. I often think about what this mountain might have meant to Betty. I wonder how long she labored on *Indian Summer* and what she was doing in her life at the time. I want to tell her that her painting gives me a contented feeling, and that on days when I'm squirreled away at my desk working toward a deadline, it calls out to me, warning me not to forget about the world beyond my computer screen.

Over time, I've developed an attachment to the painting and to Betty. I've stopped worrying about whether the painting is good or not. It speaks to me, and that's enough. I can almost convince myself that I had hiked with Betty to the spot where she painted

Indian Summer. We'd sat on a rock and ate bread and cheese, and afterwards she set up her canvas and I fed breadcrumbs to the birds. But this is magical thinking—Betty does not know I exist, and I know remarkably little about her. I think of her each time I look at her paintings or pass by her house, yet I've resisted opportunities to learn more about her life and her fate. One day I spied a friend's car in Betty's driveway, and since then I've meant to ask about Betty, but something always stops me.

Standing in my laundry room gazing at the droopy sunflowers, I understand why I don't seek news of Betty, even as the logical part of me knows that she has surely died by now. In the primitive sketch before me, I recognize Betty's intention, the beauty her mind envisioned but her fingers struggled to portray. Betty's crudely drawn sunflowers expose the gap between the world we wish for and the world we get. Even as the world she was stuck with slowly destroyed her, Betty refused to let go of its beauty. Nothing in my power could stop Betty from vanishing, but in caring for this painting, I can keep her defiant act alive.

Publication Credits

"Good Circulation" by John Clayton was published in *Horizon Air Magazine*, October 2005, and in slightly different form as "Garage Sales Lead to Déjà Vu All Over Again" in *High Country News*, July 24, 2006.

Material from "Things the Color of Stone" by Jack Collom was included in *The Alphabet of the Trees: A Guide to Nature Writing*, edited by Christian McEwen and Mark Statman. New York: Teachers and Writers Collaborative, 2000.

A version of "Blacktop Cuisine" by Michael Engelhard was published in the *San Francisco Chronicle*, December 3, 2006.

"Why I Love the Dump" by Chavawn Kelley was published in *Northern Lights*, winter 1997.

Material from "It Keeps the Heart Happy" by Laura Pritchett was published in *5280* and *High Country News*.

"Throwing Out the Dishwater," by Susan J. Tweit was published in *High Country News*, May 2004.